All About the Stars

All About the Stars

By Anne Terry White

Illustrated by Marvin Bileck

RANDOM HOUSE
NEW YORK

ELEVENTH PRINTING

 Published in New York by Random House, Inc., and simultaneously in Toronto, Canada, by Random House of Canada, Ltd.

MANUFACTURED IN THE U.S.A.

LIBRARY OF CONGRESS CATALOG CARD NUMBER: 53-6281

For Deborah Ann and her cousins

Stevie

Larry

Mitchie

Contents

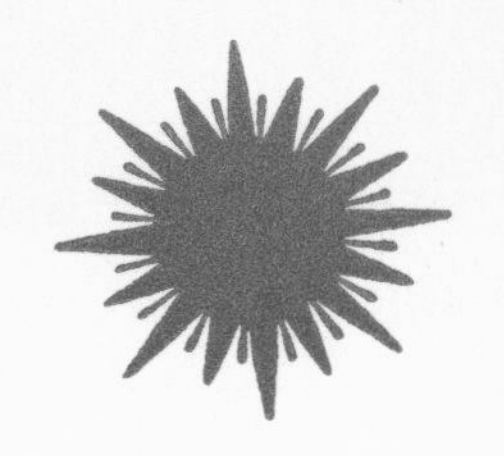

1.

Where in the World Are We?

There is always something exciting about seeing your first star in the dimness of the early evening. Once you see it, the keen sparkle of this first star is so bright, so insistent, that it seems like a light which was just switched on. Many simple people of long ago thought that heavenly spirits actually did flit across the sky lighting every star in turn. We cannot blame them. It seems that way to us, but we know better. The stars have been there all day. They always shine day and night. The only reason we don't see them in the daytime is that the blue sky is too bright.

All About the Stars

Slowly the dark comes on, and one by one more stars appear. You begin to count them. Very soon, however, you give up. "The stars are countless," you say and stand awe-struck, head tilted back, gazing at the wonder that is the starry sky. If it is a moonless night and you are far from disturbing city lights, you know that you are looking at one of the most thrilling sights Nature has to show.

You look, and it seems to you that the sky is a great dome over your head and that the stars are attached to this mighty dome. They don't look far away—a mile or two at most. And, strangely, though some of the stars are bright and some are dim, they all look about equally near.

Some of the stars, you notice, are in groups as if they belonged together. You know these groups are called constellations (stars that go together), but you find it hard to see in them the pictures the ancients saw there. For the life of you, you can't make out either a bull or a dog or a sea monster or a lion or any of the heroes and heroines of the Greek myths. You can pick out a U or a V or a W, but that's about all. And then to the north, there's the Big Dipper—seven bright stars. You recognize the Dipper as a familiar friend because it is

One constellation seems to make the picture of a dragon

one of the few things in the sky that really does look like its name.

Now that you've located the Big Dipper, you feel more sure of yourself. You feel anchored somehow. Your eyes pass quickly from bright star to bright star to fix themselves finally on the great wonder of the heavens—a wide, but very faint, white belt stretching right across the sky and dividing it into two equal parts. You know it is the Milky Way. You have heard there are millions of stars in it. But strain your eyes as hard as you can, you can't make them out individually. "Why are there more stars in the Milky Way than farther off?" you wonder.

And then you think: "This earth on which I stand is also a heavenly body. It, too, is somewhere in the sky among those stars. But where? It belongs with the sun, I know, because the earth goes around the sun, but the sunset over there in the west and the stars overhead look ever so much nearer."

It seems to you that you know so little about the stars. And yet your thoughts reveal how much more you know than the wisest men of long ago. For it never occurred to them to ask, "Where in the world are we?" They all took it for granted that our earth is the center of the universe and that the sun, the moon and the stars exist to serve it—the sun to give us light by day and the moon and stars by night. Why, who could doubt it? Couldn't everyone see that the sun rose in the east, traveled over the earth, and set in the west? Didn't the moon follow us around? Didn't the stars rise in the east and set in the west just like the sun?

We all know better now. We know that the sun only *appears* to rise and set. We know that the stars only *appear* to circle the earth. We know it is the turning of the earth that makes it seem as if the sun and the stars were going around the earth.

But let's not give ourselves too much credit. We aren't wiser than the men of old. Nearly all of us know more than the ancients did. But, in part, that is because we stand on their shoulders—we add our knowledge to theirs. Besides that, for more than 300 years now, we have had a wonderful instrument called the telescope. The telescope has made it possible for us to see many more heavenly bodies and to see them much closer. And that, you will soon find out, is a very great advantage.

Looking through the telescope, putting this and that

together, hitting now and again on some great law of Nature, and doing a lot of difficult figuring, astronomers have come to know quite a lot about the sun, moon and stars. Scientists today can draw us maps of the moon that spaceship explorers could use. Astronomers are on such familiar terms with the sun that they can minutely describe the spots that appear on its face. They know how big the stars are, what they are made of, how hot they are, how heavy, how fast and in what direction they are moving. Astronomers can pick out the stars which are close to us and those that are farther away. They can even answer the question you were asking a little while ago—they have even worked out the place in the heavens which our own earth occupies!

Look up at the Milky Way. That mysterious white belt is home ground to us. It belongs to us; we belong to it. The sun and the earth and the planets are all part of that luminous path that divides the heavens in half. The Milky Way is our home in the sky.

2.

Around and Around

Directly overhead the stars in the night sky do look nearer than the sun which, a little while ago, sank in the west. But we know it only seems so. The stars are infinitely farther away. We know that because we see them only as points of light whereas the sun appears to us as a disk.

Nearness causes that. The sun is very near. It is our own private star. All the other suns, which we call stars, are so far away that even through our biggest telescopes they never look like anything but points of light. The stars are so far away that light from the nearest of them takes four and one-third years to reach us. And light travels faster than anything else in all creation. It will go almost eight times around the earth in a second. So, in comparison with the nearest star, the sun is a stone's throw away. The sun is so near that its light can span the distance between us in just a little over eight minutes.

Certainly, of all the objects in the heavens, the sun is the most impressive. No wonder that long ago people worshiped it as a god! No wonder they believed the sun moved around the earth as a good caretaker moves around his domain to see that all is well! It is easy enough to fall into such error. We ourselves have a hard time believing it is the earth that does the moving.

Common sense tells us that something as big and heavy as the earth can't move. But we know we can't trust our eyes or our sense of balance in that sort of thing. We know the earth is turning, spinning completely around every twenty-four hours. The turning is so smooth that we don't get any sensation of motion at all.

For everything on earth is moving along with us, including the air and clouds that belong to the earth. It is only when we observe the sun and the stars that we recognize the fact of motion. For motion cannot be detected except in relation to something that is standing still or moving at a different rate of speed. Everyone has had the experience of being on a train that is standing next to another train and suddenly seeing that other train start to slide quietly back. Then we have looked out the window on the other side and, seeing houses and trees left behind, have realized that it is our train that has started—the other train isn't moving at all.

Without the least jerk, without the least effort, the earth rolls on through space. When the place where we live swings around where the light of the sun can strike it, we see the sun seem to rise in the east and it is day. When we roll far enough over out of the sun's light, we see the sun seem to go down in the west and it is night.

Day and night, night and day. Endlessly the earth spins. It started out that way over 3,000 million years ago. It will continue to spin that way for millions of years to come. It will not slow down one whole second in 100,000 years.

Tireless, effortless, what is the endless journey like? And how does it affect us who must be taken along on the trip?

We said the sun is very near the earth. But that is only in comparison with the stars. Actually the sun is millions of miles away—93 million to be exact, or almost exact; for the distance varies a little. It varies because the path which the earth takes around the sun is not a perfect circle but an ellipse—a slightly flattened circle—so that the distance to the sun is different at different points on the route. Besides, the sun, instead of being in the exact center of the ellipse, is a little off to one side.

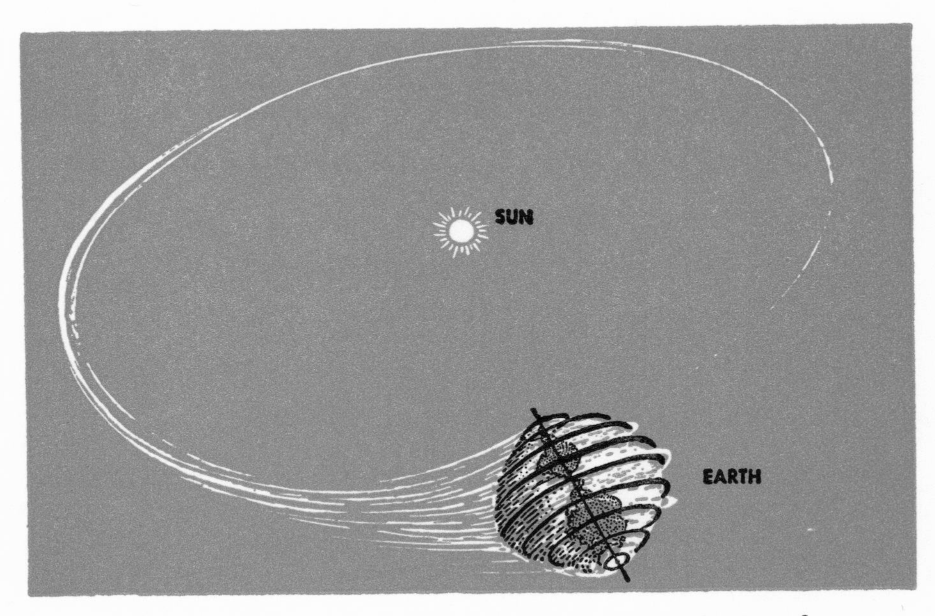

The earth's path around the sun is not a perfect circle.

Naturally, it is much, much farther than 93 million miles around the sun. It takes the earth, spinning along at 67,000 miles an hour, 365¼ days to complete that tremendous journey. That is, before it gets back to its starting point, the earth turns over 365¼ times. And when it has got around, we say, "Another year has passed." For that is what we mean by a year—one 600-million-mile trip around the sun.

And the seasons? What about them? Is the unequal distance from the sun the reason for them?

It is very natural to think so, but that's not at all the way it works. The reason for the difference between summer and winter is something altogether different. It is the way the earth tilts to one side as it spins. All the time our earth-top is spinning around the sun, it is sagging over on one side, leaning over at an angle of 23½ degrees. In spite of this, the North Pole always points toward the same place (although in the long run this place slowly shifts among the stars). This means that sometimes one pole and sometimes the other is turned part way toward the sun. When the North Pole is tipped *toward* the sun, the part of the world in which we live has summer. When the North Pole is tipped *away* from the sun, we have winter.

As a whole, of course, the earth gets about the same amount of the sun's heat every month. For when it's winter in one place, it's summer in another. How much heat any particular place gets during that month, however, depends upon its place on the globe. In December of each year the North Pole of the earth is tilted away from the sun. So up there the sun doesn't shine at all that month. In the United States it rises late, well south of east, and doesn't get very high even at noon. The days are short, the nights are long. And the air is cold —cold because the sun's rays, instead of beating right down on us, strike the earth at an angle.

Six months later, in June, the earth has swung around to the other side of its path; and the North Pole is tipped toward the sun. Up on the top of the earth people rejoice because the long night is over. The sun goes round and round in the sky; it is always above the horizon; it never sets at all now. Even as far south as Seattle, Washington, the days are sixteen hours long, and all over the United States it is the pleasant summertime. At noon the sun is high. It beats almost straight down on us.

What happens in the spring and fall?

Between summer and winter, the earth points neither to nor away from the sun. It just tilts sideways. On

March 21st the sun beats straight down on the equator and we have spring. On September 22nd the sun beats straight down on the equator and we have fall.

The tilting of the earth makes all the difference. The way it is, only twice a year are day and night just as long—on March 21st and September 22nd. If the earth stood up straight instead of sagging, it would be that way all the time—every day all over the world would be twelve hours long, and so would every night. The sun would always rise exactly in the east and climb to the same height in the sky. The height to which it climbed would depend on one thing only—how far to the north or south of the equator you happened to live. And every place on earth would have its own unchanging climate. There would be no summer and no winter anywhere, no spring and no fall.

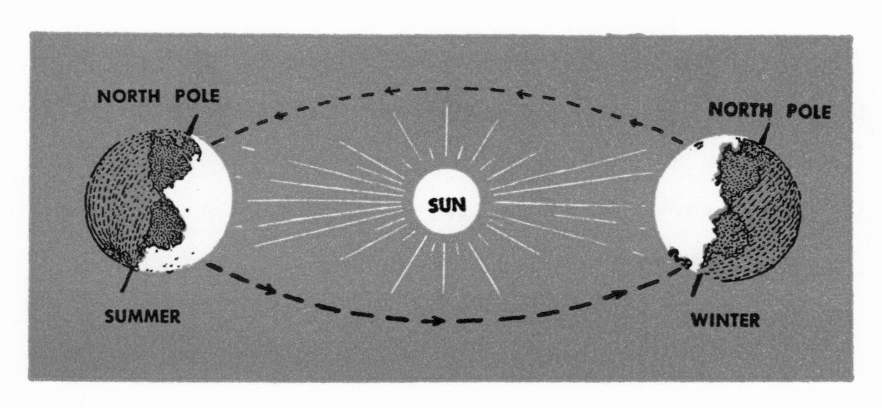

In North America summer days are long and warm.

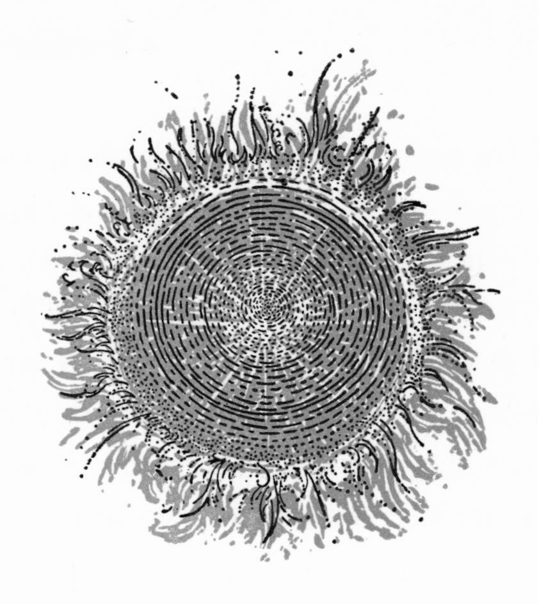

3.

Portrait of the Sun

We are used to thinking of our earth with its mighty oceans and vast continents as a pretty big globe—7,900 miles through the center, 25,000 miles around the equator. How big is it compared with the sun? A quarter as big? A tenth?

The earth is insignificant in comparison. You could pack 1,300,000 earths into the sun.

But figures of such size are hard to imagine. Suppose we could shrink the sun and the earth to a thousand-millionth of their size. Then the sun would become a ball five feet in diameter. The earth would be the size of a very small marble. It would be spinning 450 feet away—where we could just barely make it out.

That's how big the sun is. That's how small the earth is. And we, little people who make our home on a tiny marble, are completely dependent on the five-foot ball that keeps us forever prisoner circling around it.

For the sun is the big astronomical fact in our lives. It is the sun that gives us light. It is the sun that gives us heat. By causing evaporation, the sun makes the rain come down. By heating land and water unequally, it causes the winds to blow. The sun makes food for the plants and they, in turn, feed the animals and us. And the sun gives us the base of power. For wood and coal and petroleum and falling water are all of the sun's making.

What a terrific amount of heat and light the sun pours forth to accomplish all this! And yet the amount the earth catches is just a tiny fraction of the sun's radiation of heat in all directions. The heat of the sun is so great that the hottest fire is cold in comparison. At the surface the sun's heat measures 11,000° Fahrenheit. Nothing can be made that hot on earth for more than a fraction of a second. And still, inside the sun the temperature is much higher. It measures 29 million degrees Fahrenheit.

Every second the sun pours out into space over four million tons of energy. And "tons" is not just a figure of speech as we use it here. For even the light from an electric bulb has a little weight, though too little to measure, and sunlight really is measured in tons. Of those millions of tons the earth gets four pounds a second. The pounds add up to 173 tons a day. That may not sound like much after all the big figures we have been quoting. But if we had to pay for the light and heat we get from the sun for nothing, it would cost us $1,700,000,000,000 an hour. And that is too big a figure for most of us to read, let alone understand.

But what keeps the sun going? We know that a fire dies if it isn't fed. We know that we ourselves waste away if we don't eat. If the sun isn't getting anything from outside and is losing four million tons of energy a second, why doesn't it grow cold?

The answer is: it will in time. However, that time is so infinitely far away that nobody need bother his head about it. The sun is indeed using up its own substance to make its radiant heat. But the sun is so big and is using its substance so sparingly that it is in no danger of getting cold. The sun is extremely economical. It is using up only one million-millionth $\left(\frac{1}{1,000,000,000,000}\right)$ of its resources a year. So, although the sun has been shining for several thousand million years, it is still extremely hot. It is so glowing hot that at the distance of 93 million miles it dazzles our eyes. We cannot bear to look at it.

What, then, is the sun made of? Surely nothing so hot as the sun can remain a solid!

Surely not. The sun is a tremendous globe of glowing gas. On earth all the gases we know are much, much lighter than any liquid. On the sun, however, the gas particles are packed so tightly that on the average they are heavier than water. And they are never at

Fountains of glowing gas shoot out from the sun for miles.

rest. They are tumbling and flaring and spurting like geysers. To the naked eye, the face of the sun appears as a neat disk with clean-cut edges. But that's because it is so bright that we cannot see its features clearly.

We used to have to wait till a total eclipse came along to see these great fountains of gas flaring out at the edges. Then we would realize what commotion there is on the sun. Now, through a special eclipse-making telescope, we can see the sun's plumes any time. We can sometimes see fountains of glowing gas shooting out hundreds of thousands of miles. And beyond that we can see the mysterious, silvery halo of the corona, the sun's outer atmosphere, which is not like our atmosphere at all. It is very hot and very thin and contains vapors of iron and nickel and calcium. At times of total eclipse it can be traced out to several million miles beyond the sun.

Tumbling and shooting out and falling back in, the restless gases that make up the sun are at the same time rotating continually. For, like the earth, the sun is always turning though very, very slowly. How can we tell that? By watching the spots on the sun's surface. The sunspots don't stand still. They move all in one direction.

It may be a disappointment to you to hear that the sun is not perfect, and it was certainly a shock to the world when the great Italian astronomer, Galileo, pointed it out. But there are certainly dark spots on the sun, and once in a great while, even with the naked eye you can see them, provided you look through a piece of smoked glass to cut down the glare. They are pretty big, too. They have to be more than a thousand miles across to be seen at all. But sometimes they are very much bigger. In 1947 there was one that had an area of five thousand million square miles. More than a hundred earths could have been swallowed up in it.

Usually you see the sunspots in groups, and when one is visible all by itself you can be pretty sure it's the last of a lot that have disappeared. For sunspots break out in a group here, a group there. First they get bigger. Then, after a week or so, generally they die away. But as you watch them moving along day after day, it becomes clear that the sun turns, though not just like the earth; for the spots near the middle move faster than the ones higher up and lower down. And this, of course, is sure proof that the sun is not solid. If it were, the whole surface would have to move together.

Watching the movement of sunspots across the face

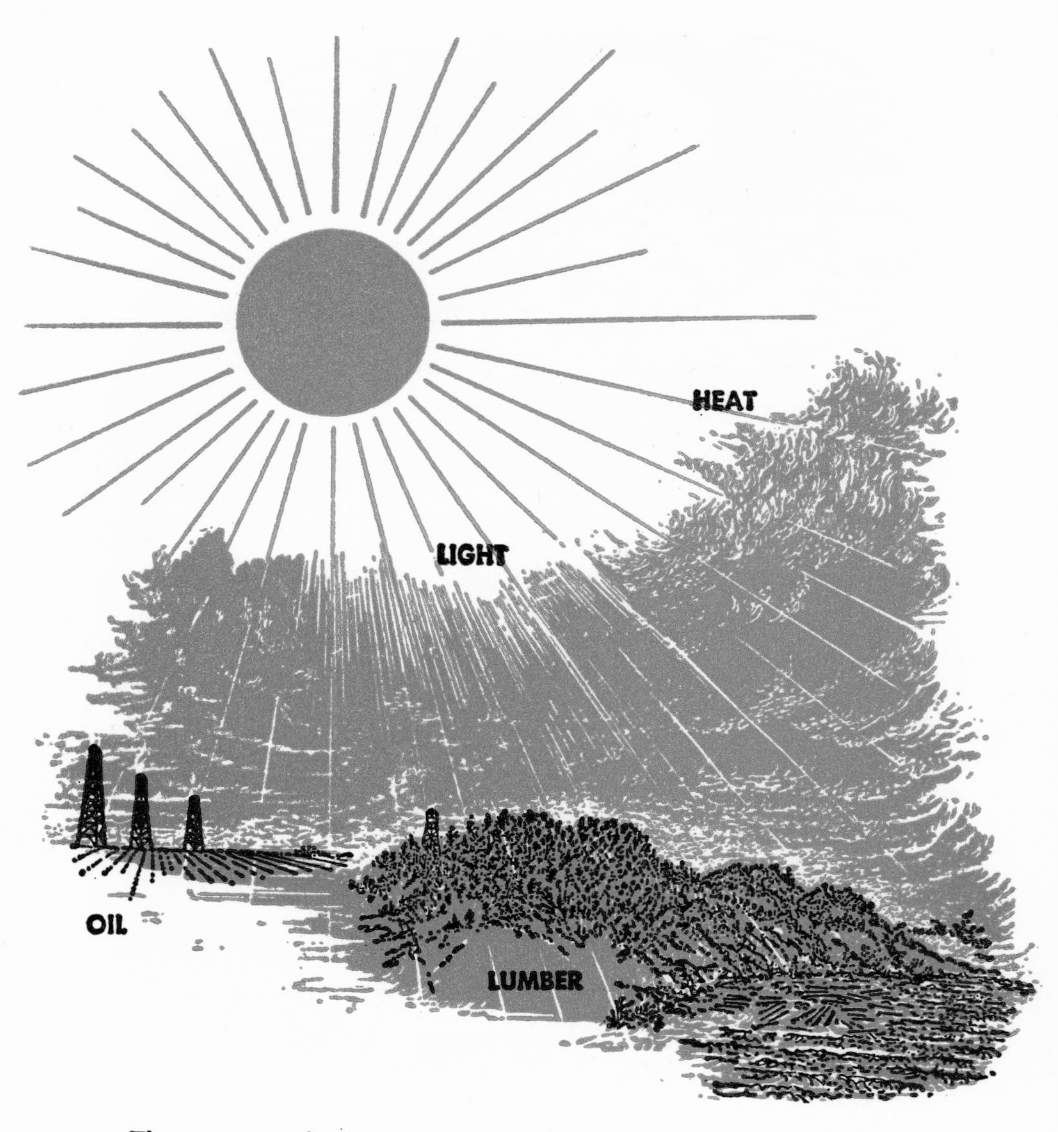

The sun provides heat and light and causes the winds to blow.

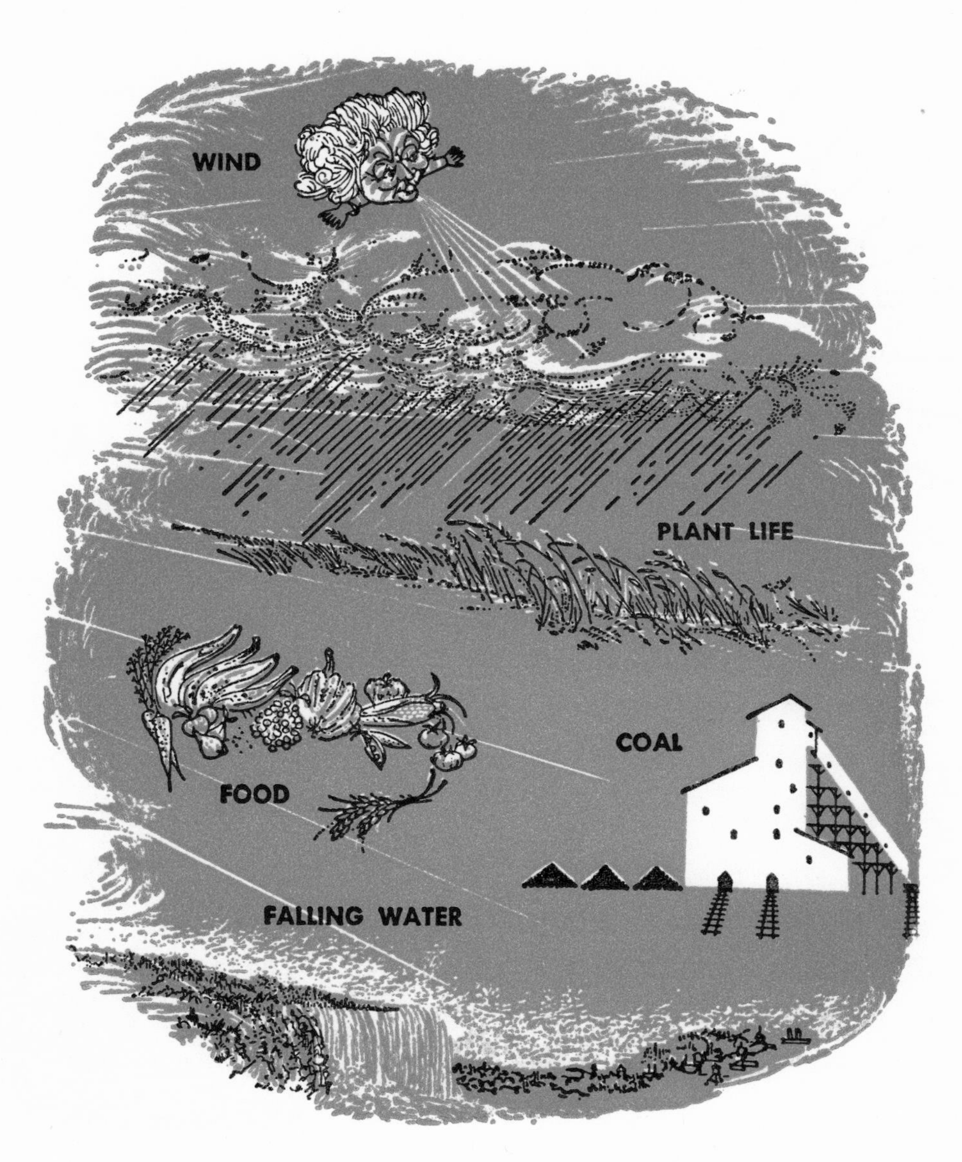

Wood, coal and petroleum are all of the sun's making.

of the sun, we have found out how long the sun's "day" is—that is, how long it takes the sun to turn completely around. We know that at the equator it takes about twenty-five days and at the poles over a month. So we can say that the sun's "day" is more than three weeks, but that it is different in different latitudes.

Of course, the sunspots aren't really dark. Nothing on a place so hot as the sun could really be dark. Set the sunspots in the sky by themselves, and they would shine like stars. The sunspots only seem dark in comparison with the clear parts. And the reason they are darker can mean just one thing—the sunspots are cooler areas. Cooler by the sun's standard, that is; for by earthly standards, they are still very hot—8,000° Fahrenheit or so.

What are these mysterious spots that come and go and rotate with the surface of the sun?

We don't know exactly. But we do know that they are something like the storms on the earth. The gases in the sunspots swirl up and down. The way they act reminds you of tornadoes except that on the sunspots there is little circular twisting.

As for the number you can see at any one time, that differs with the year. In a poor year you might see fifty groups of spots; in an active year you might see 300 or 400 groups. But here is the curious thing. Sunspots go through a sort of cycle. About every eleven years there comes a big sunspot year. Then there are fewer again till the next big year.

From all this coming and going of sunspots one thing is sure. The sun, which to us appears so peaceful and tranquil as it rises and sets, is actually the scene of constant violence. In addition to the constant boiling up of light and heat from down below, there is a big-scale, longer rhythm in the sun. About every eleven years comes a high point and the spot break-outs repeat themselves. Only in each cycle the pattern of spots changes—they appear in different places on the sun.

Naturally, what we want to know is how all this affects us. The sun rules us so completely that it seems any change on the sun should make a difference to us. Is it colder when the sunspots are many and warmer when they are few?

Strangely enough, the answer is "no." Sunspots have no direct effect on our weather. But they do have an influence on earth. Often when a large group is crossing the sun, the earth has a magnetic storm. We have trouble with our radios. And the northern lights are especially brilliant.

Such is the portrait of the sun. It seems very different from our own cool, solid, gentle earth with its grass and trees and clouds. And yet the materials of which earth and sun are made are the same. Oxygen, nitrogen, carbon, iron, sulphur, sodium—all the elements we know on earth are present in the sun. There is an important difference, however. These elements are not there in the same proportions. Only two are found in quantity on the sun—the two lightest, hydrogen and helium.

Indeed the sun is practically all hydrogen and helium. As someone has put it, of the other elements there isn't much more than "a smell." And that is just as it should be so far as we on earth are concerned. The secret of the sun's power lies in hydrogen and helium. It is by changing hydrogen into helium that the sun keeps going. Every time it converts four atoms of hydrogen into one atom of helium, the sun gets a little more energy. Heat and light are produced. It is just as though hydrogen were "fuel" which the sun is "burning." It is just as though helium is the "ashes" that are left. Some of the other elements seem to be needed to keep the process going, but they aren't used up. Only the hydrogen grows less and less.

But that need alarm no one. We know the sun has been shining just as now for hundreds of millions of years at least because there has been life on earth that long. And still the sun is mostly hydrogen. Have no fear! The sun will keep on shining for thousands of millions of years to come.

4.

Our Next-Door Neighbor

Look up at the full moon, and it seems to be a disk about as big as the sun. But that, again, is only because the moon is so near us. It is less than a quarter of a million miles away. Compared to the sun, the moon is our next-door neighbor. The moon is our closest companion. It follows us wherever we go. It keeps circling around us as we spin about the sun.

We know a great deal about the moon—in fact, more than we know about some places on earth. That is, we know about the side we see. For the moon takes as long to make a complete turn as it takes to go around the earth. Consequently it shows us the same face all the time. We shall have to wait till a space ship gets around to the back before we know what the moon other side looks like.

The moon is really quite a small object compared to the earth, which is fifty times as large. And for all it looks so romantic as it sails through the clouds or casts a silvery beam upon the water, it isn't at all beautiful like our earth. It has neither grass nor trees nor life of any kind. It has no air. It has no water. And it is deadly dull. Hardly anything happens on the moon, nothing ever changes; for it is as dead as any world can be. The moon is burned out, done for. The only excitement is the occasional swift fall of a meteorite that tears up the dusty surface.

As you well know, the moon is not always "full." How much of it we see depends on where the moon is on its path around the earth. Sometimes we see no moon at all. That happens when the sun, earth and moon are lined up and the moon is in the middle. At such times the sun shines only on the back of the moon, and the side that faces us is dark. We call it *new moon* then. Sometimes the sun, earth and moon are lined up with the earth in the middle. Then we see the whole face of the moon lit up. It is *full moon.* At other times we see just half of the moon's face or less.

Well now, let us follow the changing moon with our eyes. Let us watch it through its phases.

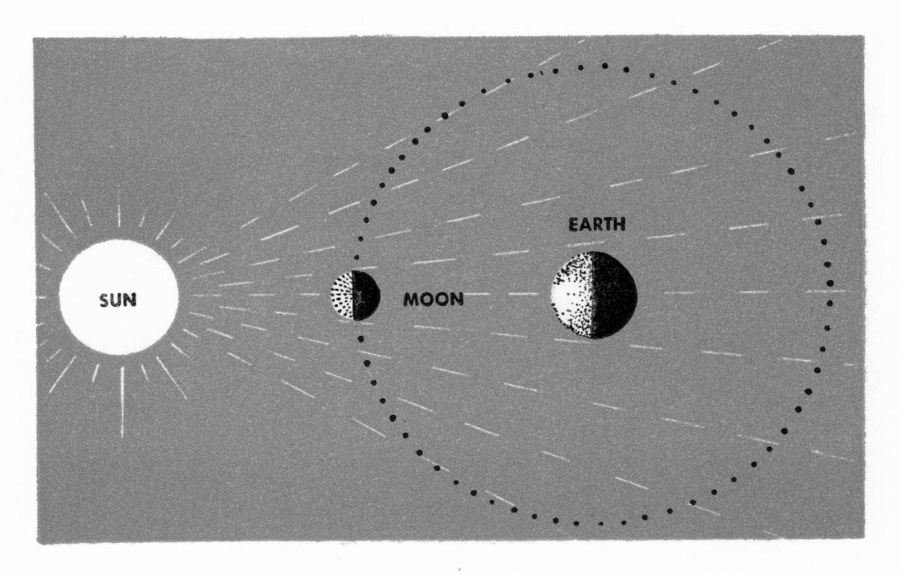

When it is "new moon," we see no moon at all.

Two or three days after new moon we look into the western sky at twilight, and there we see a crescent. It is slim and fair and wonderfully fresh looking. Because the earth is always turning, the crescent, like everything else in the sky, appears to move from east to west. But if there is a bright star near the moon, we can easily see that this is not its true direction. Even in an hour's time we can see that the moon is working its way east against the background of the stars, moving about its own width every hour.

Sometimes when the moon is young like that, we

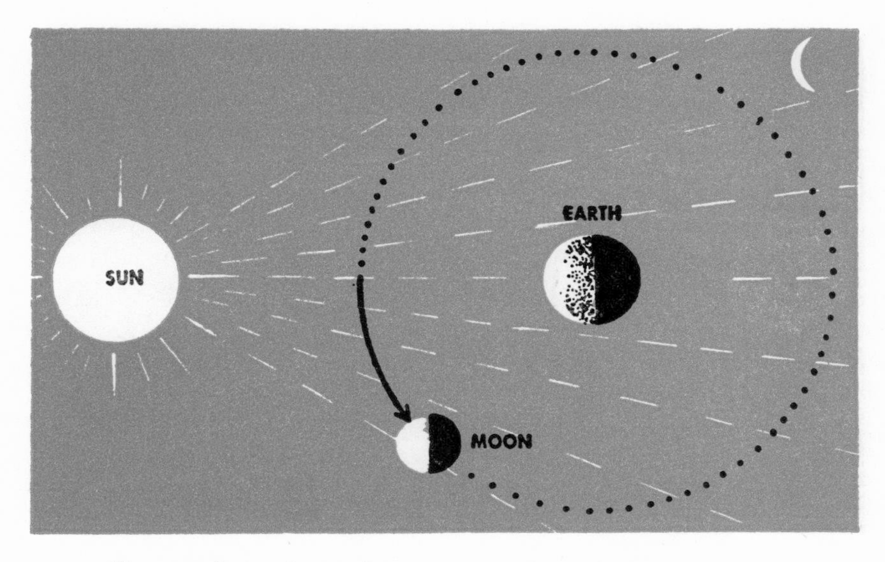

Two or three days after new moon, we see a crescent.

can see a strange sight. Faintly, very faintly, we can see the part of the moon that is *not* lit up by the sun. Poets have called this effect "the old moon in the new moon's arms," and for us it has a special fascination. We know that the light by which we see the dark part of the moon is our own earth-light. Our own planet is reflecting the sun's light and is shining so brightly that it lets us see into the deep shadow of the dark side of the moon. If we were up on the moon, we would be able to read a newspaper by this earth-light. We would find it fifty times stronger than the brightest

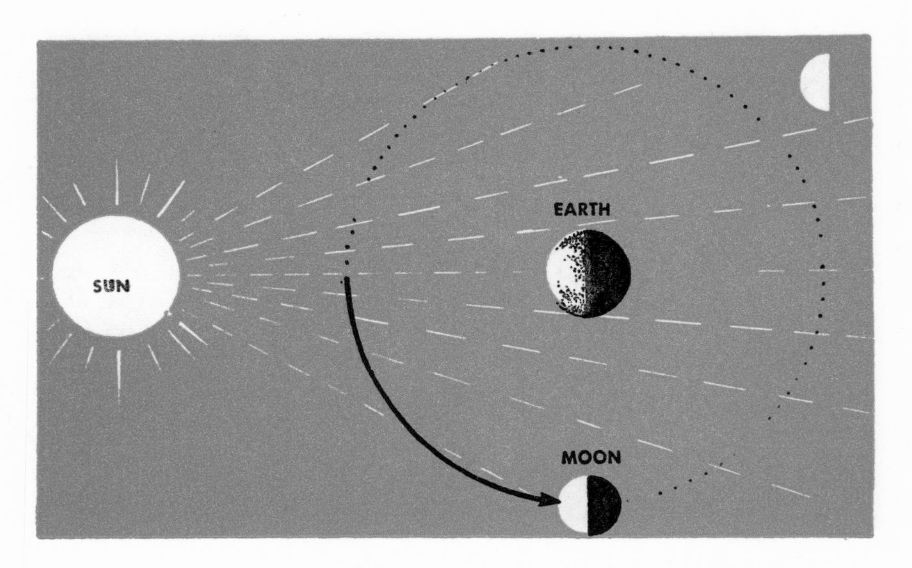

When the moon is at first quarter, it looks like half a pie.

moonlight.

But the old moon doesn't stay long in the new moon's arms. By the time the moon is five days old, we can no longer see the reflection of our earth-light. And now we notice that the inside of the crescent moon is a little straighter. Our slim and dainty crescent is gaining weight. After seven days it has grown into a stubby half-a-pie. Now we say the moon is at *first quarter* because by this time it is one quarter of the way around the earth.

Another week, and our satellite has grown to full

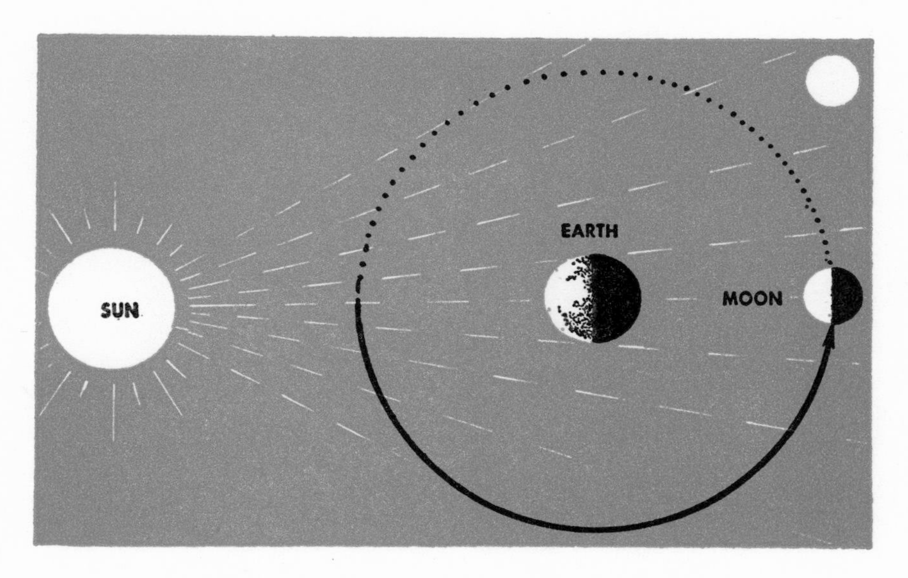

In another week our satellite has grown to full moon.

moon. It is very bright and shining now; it rules the sky; it dims the stars. It is the moon in all its glory. But a few days later we notice that the western side of our full moon seems to be getting smaller. From now on, night by night, we see it dwindle. As it approaches *last quarter* at the end of the third week, we see that it looks as it did at first quarter. But now it is the left-hand part that is bright. Three-fourths of the moon's journey is over. And now the last quarter shrinks and shrinks till again we have a crescent. Finally, once more the earth and moon are lined up with the sun. Twenty-nine and a half days have passed since last new moon, and now the cycle begins again.

We have said that it is either new moon or full moon when earth and moon are lined up with the sun. But really we should have said "on the same line as the sun." Because, from our point of view, the moon usually passes either over or under the sun. When the moon, or a part of it, really does get exactly in line with the sun, we have what we call an eclipse. For a little while the whole sun, or a part of it, is covered up by the moon. That happens at least twice a year, but we can't always see it from where we are.

The most exciting eclipse by far is the one where the whole sun gets blacked out by the moon. We call that a *total eclipse* of the sun. Then sudden darkness comes even at noon, and people who don't understand what is happening are terrified. Animals get uneasy; birds think night is falling and go to roost.

A total eclipse of the sun is always front-page news, and if the eclipse can be seen from where we are, everybody drops whatever he is doing and runs out to watch. From a high place the moon's shadow can be seen as it

During an eclipse of the sun, the moon blots out the sun.

sweeps across the surface of the earth. You can clearly see it on the ground even if the eclipse comes at high noon. The shadow is not very large—never over 166 miles wide where it touches the earth. It comes racing across the ground at more than 1,000 miles an hour. Looking up at the sun through a piece of smoked glass, we can see the bright disk being swallowed bit by bit. In a little while the last sliver is covered up. An eerie gloom falls on the land. It is not the darkness of dark night nor even of a bright moonlight night. And yet the brightest stars suddenly appear, and we can see the corona glowing like silver all about the sun.

The eclipse doesn't last long. A total eclipse can never last more than seven minutes and forty seconds. That is because the moon, even at its closest, cannot appear much bigger than the sun. It can never much more than just fit over the sun. And besides, the moon moves all the time; so it can't shut out the sun's light very long.

Since the shadow path of the moon is so narrow and can fall anywhere on the earth at all, you might have to wait more than 200 years to see a total eclipse of the sun in your town. Astronomers naturally wouldn't think of waiting for an eclipse to come to them. They go to it. They know exactly from what place it can be seen because they can calculate precisely how the shadow will cross the earth.

Often they travel thousands of miles to see a total eclipse. But you can see a *partial eclipse* without taking a trip. Every year or so you can see the sun with what looks like a bite taken out of it by the moon. That is when earth, moon and sun are *nearly* lined up.

But here is a curious thing. Even when sun, moon

and earth are *exactly* lined up, we don't always get a total eclipse. We get an eclipse with just a little circle of sun showing all around the edge. We call that an *annular* or *ring eclipse*. It happens because some of the time the moon isn't big enough to cover the whole sun. And the reason is that our distance from the sun and from the moon changes. Sometimes the moon looks bigger, and sometimes it looks smaller. At times when it looks smallest, it can't quite cover the sun.

Of course, it isn't always the sun's turn to get eclipsed. Sometimes sun, moon and earth get on an exact line, and the earth instead of the moon is in the middle. Then we get an eclipse of the moon. The huge cone of shadow cast by the earth falls on the full moon. At such times there is never a complete blackout, however. Some of the sun's light is bent into the shadow by the earth's atmosphere so that the moon can still be seen though it is eclipsed. Usually the moon shows a dull red even in the middle of the eclipse. The eclipse of the moon is not so spectacular as even a partial eclipse of the sun. But at least it can be watched from anywhere—provided the moon is above our horizon at the time.

What does the moon really look like?

Until we had the telescope, people imagined all sorts of things about the moon. The dark spots that make it look so much like a face and that we call the man in the moon kept everybody wondering and guessing. Was the moon perhaps a great mirror that reflected the continents and oceans of the earth? Did we see the map of the earth spread out on the moon?

We don't have to wonder any more. Even with small telescopes it is possible to see what the moon is really like. We can see mountains as high as the Rockies with deep straight valleys running through them. We can see cliffs, wide-walled craters, and vast, dark areas which, at one time, were believed to be seas. Now we know there is no water on the moon.

The most puzzling things are the craters of the moon. They are of all sizes up to 100 miles and more across, though most of them measure between five and twenty miles across. They are far larger than any craters we find on the earth. Around each is a high mountain wall. On the floor of a great many craters there is a mountain peak. Sometimes there is a crater within a crater. Altogether there are over 30,000 craters on the moon.

What are they? What made them? We call them craters. But were they formed by volcanoes as was at

The mountains of the moon are high and rugged.

first supposed? We are not at all sure now. Perhaps some—perhaps all—of the craters were made by falling masses of metal or stone which exploded when they struck the moon.

The day may not be too far off when human feet will climb into one of those craters and human hands will touch those walls. For though some people still laugh at the idea, a visit to the moon is no longer a fantastic dream. The cost would, of course, be immense. But by using three-stage rockets and a space station it could be done. Until we have much better rocket fuels than we have today, we won't attempt the trip. But when we do have enough power, we surely will be able to get away from the earth, land gently on the moon, be launched from there, and return to the earth.

Unquestionably it will be a tremendous victory to land on the moon. But our rocket explorers will be very glad to set their feet on earth again—our own pleasant earth where there is air to breathe and water to drink, where we don't boil in the daytime and freeze at night, where the winds blow, and where we can hear our friends when they speak to us.

Our explorers will report that during the day—which

on the moon is over fourteen of our days long—it was insufferably hot. The sun beat down so that the rocks got hotter than boiling water. But in the afternoon it began to get cold. And by the time the sun went down, it was below freezing. During the very first hours of the night—which on the moon is over fourteen of our nights long—it got to be 150° below freezing, colder than any place on earth ever gets. Our explorers will say that they found the sky inky black even in the daytime and that they saw stars always shining very blue and twinkling not at all. And they will tell us about the weird, oppressive stillness in that airless world.

When our triumphant explorers come back with their story, they will surely prick the bubble of the hopes which, for years, have been fed us by silly books about the moon. The moon is not a place where there is ever likely to be a real-estate boom. The moon is out of the running as a place even to spend a week end. The moon is a has-been. We cannot look to it ever to be of any more use to us than it is right now. In shedding its gentle light on the earth and in raising the tides on our oceans, the moon is doing for us all that it can or ever will.

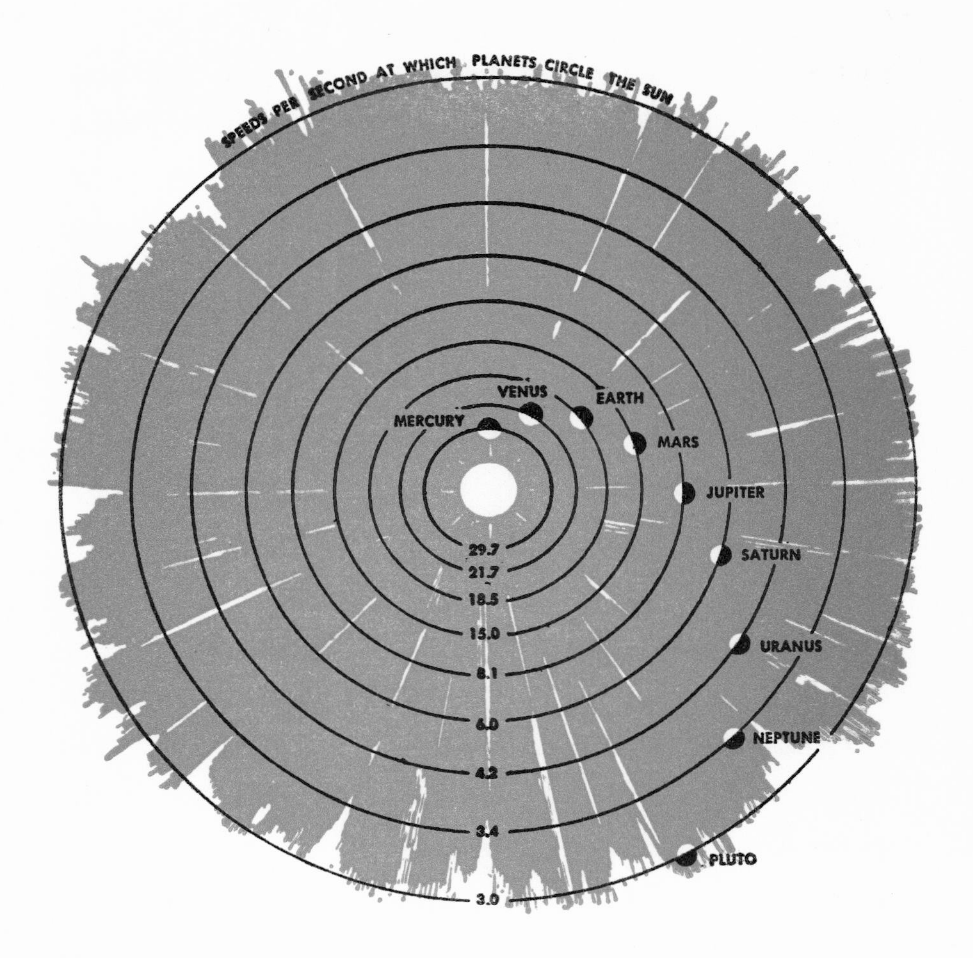

5.

Traffic Laws of the Sky

Wise men watched the heavens even 5,000 years ago to see what the stars were doing. They saw the stars rise in the east and set in the west. Each night they saw the stars do the same thing, only do it four minutes earlier. The minutes added up. After a few weeks the ancients noticed that the stars they had seen rise in the east late at night were well up in the eastern sky as soon as it was dark enough to see the stars at all. The stars they had seen in the west when it first got dark were all the way down behind the horizon by the time the sun had set.

After a few months they realized that the sky had gradually changed. They weren't seeing the same stars in the spring that they had seen in the winter. They didn't realize that these new stars were those that had been shining in the daytime before. But they clearly saw that when a year had passed, the stars were all back in their places. The stars were always in the same places at the same time. They never seemed to change. They were never any farther from, or any closer to, any other stars. For this reason, the men of old called them the *fixed stars.*

But these wise men also noticed that not every one of the stars was a fixed star. Among the bright lights in the sky were a few, a very few, that did move against the background of the others. The ancients called them *planets,* meaning *wanderers.* They knew five such

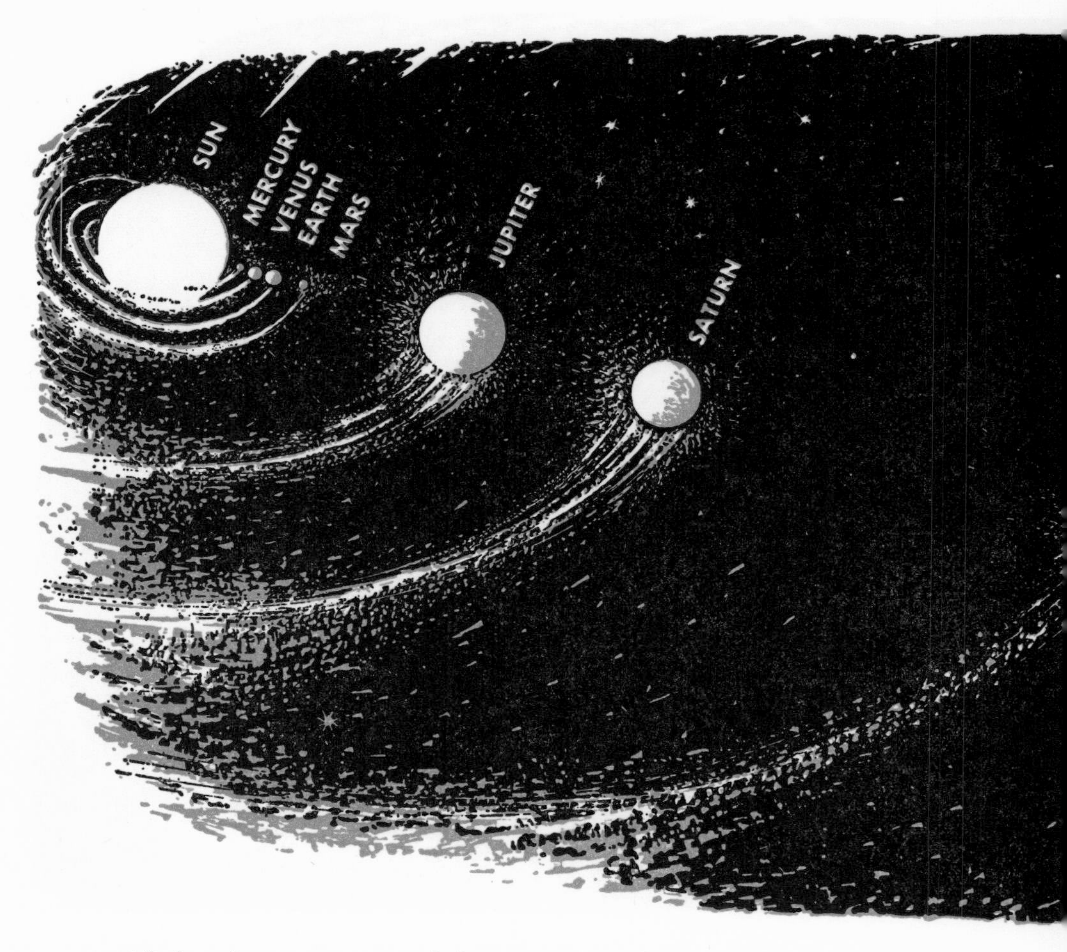

All the planets go around the sun just as the earth does.

planets. They called the planets Mercury, Venus, Mars, Jupiter and Saturn. The moon and the sun they also put in the same class. All of these, they believed, moved around the earth. And so, they imagined, did the stars. They never guessed that the earth itself is a wanderer.

We know now that the fixed stars don't really stand

Each planet moves faster as it comes closer to the sun.

still. The stars do move and shift their positions. They appear to do it so slowly, however, that in a lifetime one cannot notice any difference.

As for the planets, we know that they are the earth's brothers and sister and go around the sun just as the earth does. Together they make a family. And they have distinct family characteristics. Unlike the stars, they don't shine by their own light. And unlike the stars, they show a disk—or part of one—when you look at them through the telescope.

The sun's family has grown considerably since the wise men of old singled out the five brightest planets. Three more major members have been discovered—Uranus, Neptune and Pluto. Besides these, there have been added a couple of thousand lesser ones, too many to mention individually. They go under the general name of *asteroids*. All of them travel in very nearly the same belt around the sun but at different distances from it.

The planets all behave so much alike it almost looks as if they were following certain traffic rules. They move around in the same direction—counterclockwise, opposite to the way the hands of the clock move. The path of each is an ellipse. Each planet moves faster as it comes closer to the sun and more slowly as it moves farther away. And the farther out in space the planet's path is, the slower is the speed at which the planet travels.

Planets do act according to law. And ever since the great English mathematician, Isaac Newton, pointed it out, we know what that law is. It is called *gravitation.* What it means is simply this: every object in the world exerts a pull on every other object no matter how far away it is.

Newton got his idea by seeing an apple fall from a tree. Millions of other people had seen apples fall from trees, but they had not bothered about it. Isaac Newton did; he asked why and answered his question by saying that the earth exerts a pull on the apple. He went further and said that the apple also exerts a pull on the earth. The apple exerts *the same amount of pull* on the earth, he said, as the earth does on the apple. Only the earth, being so very big, doesn't respond to the apple's pull. The apple, being so small, does respond to the earth's pull. That's why it falls to the earth. Newton called the attracting force *gravity* or *gravitation.*

We all know the earth does act as if it pulled everything toward its center. We know, for example, that we can't jump very high—the earth pulls us down. We know that we have to exert a lot of strength to lift a piano. We say it is heavy. What we mean is that the earth pulls the piano toward itself so hard that we have to struggle to get it up. We know also that if we throw a ball into the air it doesn't keep on going up. After a while it curves toward the earth and falls down. The earth pulls down the ball.

Now Newton didn't stop with the apple. Nor with a ball. He went on asking questions. Did this same law of gravitation apply to the moon? Did the earth pull the moon toward itself? He believed that if a body was given a push that started it moving through space it would travel in a straight line unless something interfered with it. Was gravitation preventing the moon from going off in a straight line through space as it wanted to do? Was the pull of the earth making the moon curve toward it? Was that why the path of the moon was in the shape of an ellipse?

He knew the size of the earth and the size of the moon. He knew how far apart they were. He knew the rates at which they were traveling. He knew also "the rate of fall"—that is, how fast a free thing like a ball will fall at the end of one second, at the end of two seconds and so on. He figured and figured. And his figures convinced him that it was as he thought. The earth did exert a pull on the moon just as it did on the ball. The amount of pull on a body, however, depended not only on its weight but also on how far away that body was. Gravitation acted so that a thing twice as far away would be pulled only a quarter as hard.

Now, the moon is sixty times as far from the earth's center as something that is on or near the earth's surface. So the moon, he figured, is being pulled with a force only $\frac{1}{3600}$ as great. That is, the moon is falling toward the earth a fraction of an inch a second. But, unlike the ball, it never does fall all the way down. It doesn't fall all the way down because it is moving so fast, trying to go in a straight line through space. It only *curves* toward the earth—that is, it only falls *around* the earth. The ellipse in which it travels is a compromise. It is a compromise between the moon's own forward motion and the pull of the earth.

Newton proved to everybody that he was right. His figuring convinced all the scientists that gravitation is the great law of the universe. It is gravitation that makes the moon go in an oval path around the earth. It is gravitation that lays down the traffic rules for the sun's family. The planets *must* travel in an ellipse around the sun. They *must* travel at the speeds they do. The nearer they are to the sun, the faster they must move; for the nearer to the sun, the greater the pull. A planet has to obey the traffic laws.

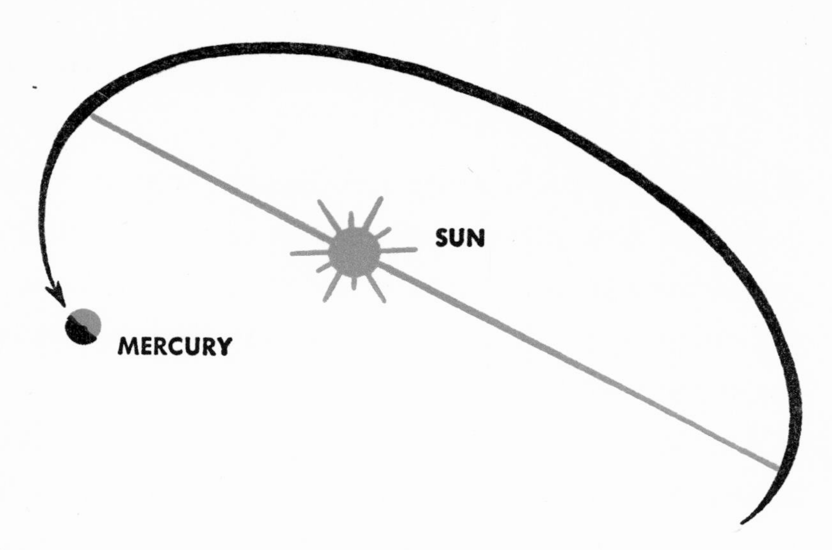

6.

Mercury

Mercury is the baby of the sun's family. It is very small indeed, only about once and a half the size of our moon. The little planet stays very close to the sun, but as its path is a quite flat ellipse and as the sun is off center, at times Mercury is very much nearer to the sun than at others. Once every three months Mercury gets 43½ million miles away from the sun, which is as far away as ever it can get. But forty-four days later it is only 28½ million miles away.

Being so close, Mercury naturally has to travel fast, and we find that it gets around the sun in eighty-eight days. That is to say, Mercury's "year" is eighty-eight of our days long. Its own day, however, is just as long as its year because Mercury acts the same way our moon does. The little planet turns around only once while it circles the sun, just as the moon turns only once as it circles the earth. And, like the moon, Mercury always shows the same face.

That means that it gets pretty hot on Mercury. The sun blazes down on it eight times as hot as on the earth, and having no chance to turn its face away, Mercury works up to 770° Fahrenheit. Which is hot enough to melt lead and tin! Out in back at the same time it is insufferably cold—400° below zero.

Naturally nothing could possibly live in such a climate. If a space ship ever goes that close to the sun, it would be effort wasted to do anything more than take a few photographs of the hot side. As for the cold side, it would perhaps be possible to land there if we had properly heated and pressurized tanklike vehicles. Explorers could travel over some of the surface and perhaps bring back samples of the rocks which cover it. But it is doubtful that anything they would see would be worth the trouble of going so far.

If explorers ever go there, they will certainly have to take their own oxygen along. For Mercury has no atmosphere. No body as small as Mercury could have air because its force of gravity wouldn't be strong enough to hold an atmosphere down.

For air is made up of gases, and the law of gases is that they expand. They will take up all the room you give them. They will go right out into space if something doesn't stop them. The only reason the earth's atmosphere hasn't expanded all the way out into space is that the earth's pull holds it down. Even so, once in

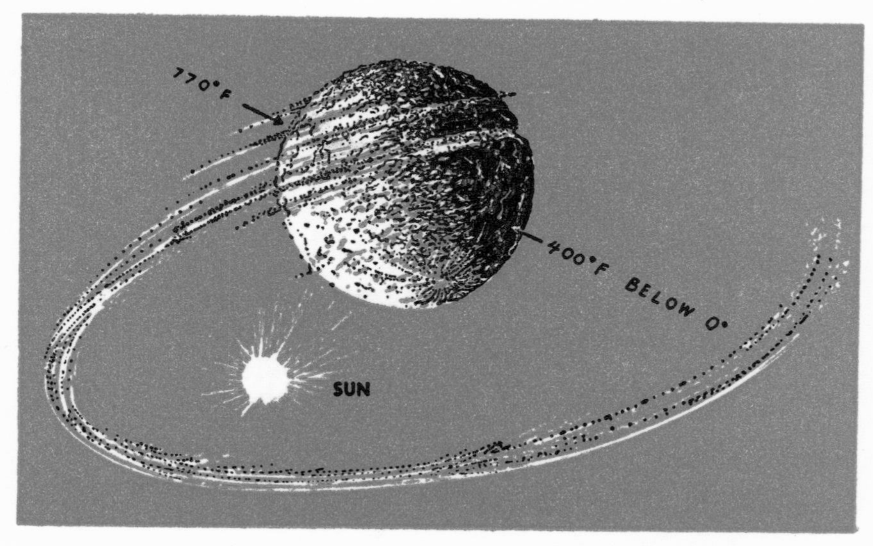

Mercury is extremely hot on the side facing the sun.

a while an atom of hydrogen does escape.

There is a saying: "Everything that goes up must come down." But that's not true. If it starts off fast enough, it doesn't have to come down. However, to escape from the earth it has to be traveling pretty fast —seven miles a second. This speed is called the *velocity of escape*. Smaller bodies have smaller velocities of escape. The velocity of escape from our moon is only one and a half miles a second. The atoms of the moon's atmosphere didn't have to be traveling very fast to get away from it. So the moon lost its air long ago.

Mercury is not much bigger than the moon. The velocity of escape from Mercury is not much more. So we know that Mercury can't hold on to its atmosphere. This, of course, means there is no water there either, for all the water would have evaporated long ago and gone off with the air.

Mercury is airless and waterless like the moon, and like the moon it has phases. Sometimes we see half of Mercury's hot face. Sometimes we see only a quarter. Sometimes we see just a slender little crescent.

It seems wonderful that the ancients ever discovered the little planet at all. For though it shines brightly, Mercury can seldom be seen with the naked eye. It is visible only for a few days about six times a year just after sunset or just before sunrise. And in the twilight and thick air near the horizon it is hard to find.

7.

Behind a Curtain of Clouds

Next beyond Mercury is Venus, the planet men sometimes call the Evening Star and sometimes the Morning Star. It is bright, beautiful and utterly mysterious.

Because Venus is at times only 26 million miles away from the earth, you would expect us to be well acquainted with our twin sister. But exactly the opposite is true—we know almost nothing of Venus. And that's for two reasons. The first is that when Venus is closest to us we see only the dark side of the planet. The second is that Venus is completely covered with clouds all the time. Our big telescopes can indeed bring Venus very close. But it's no use—we simply can't see the surface through the clouds. Occasionally, when the air is extremely still and it is daytime, we can see some markings in the covering clouds. Nothing more.

We know so little about Venus that we aren't even sure how long its day is. We know it takes the planet seven and a half of our months to get around the sun, but astronomers still wonder how long it takes Venus to turn around. We have reason to think that it may take roughly thirty times as long as the earth takes to turn. That is, a day on Venus may be as long as a month on earth. But we may be mistaken.

However, we can reason and we can calculate and we can speculate. We know that Venus is almost the size of the earth. That means its velocity of escape is almost seven miles a second. So we know that the planet has been able to hold on to an atmosphere.

But what kind of atmosphere is it? We know there is a great deal of carbon dioxide above the cloud curtain, several thousand times more than we have in our own atmosphere. Over and above that, however, we know little about Venus' atmosphere. Is there water vapor in it? Is there oxygen? If there is, we can find no trace of them high up above the cloud layer.

What about conditions on the ground?

We have to suppose it is hot there because Venus is nearer the sun. To be sure, the cloud curtain reflects back into space six-tenths of the sunlight that falls on the planet. But enough must get through to make the surface uncomfortably hot. Some astronomers think "uncomfortably" a mild term for it. They say "unbearably" hot, more than 212° Fahrenheit, which is the boiling point of water. They insist that if there is water on Venus, it must be in the form of steam.

Maybe they are right, and maybe they aren't. If there is no water, then Venus is probably a blazing hot desert. But how do we account for the clouds? If they aren't made of water droplets, what are they made of? We don't know.

In these days of talk about space travel, one of the things we are interested in finding out about Venus, of course, is whether human beings could stay alive there. Would they have to wear a special air-conditioned space suit all the time? The chances of there being people on Venus are very slim. And even these may quite disappear as we get more facts. Years before a space ship can be sent exploring, all hope of finding

Venus a friendly planet may be wiped out.

Looked at with the naked eye, Venus—which has phases like the moon and Mercury—is always far brighter than any other planet or star in the sky. It is so bright that in winter it will cast shadows of trees on the snow. It can even be seen in the daytime. In fact, it is so brilliant that when people spot it in the daytime they often get excited and report that they have seen a "flying saucer" in the bright blue sky.

Venus is seen only as an evening or a morning star. You will never see it at midnight. The bright planet either follows the sun down in the west or comes up in the east before the sun rises. If you remember where to look and then look a little earlier each evening when Venus is getting farther and farther from the setting sun, you will soon be able to find it while the sun is still above the horizon.

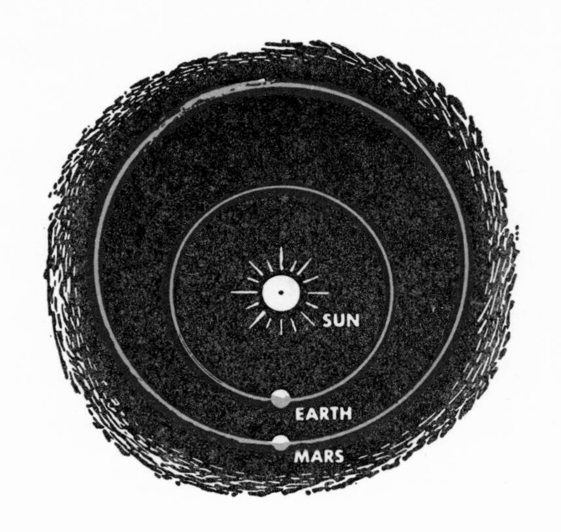

8.

Are There Intelligent Beings on Mars?

The earth comes next after Venus. And on the other side of us, 141 million miles from the sun, Mars travels along its path. Of all the planets Mars makes us the most curious. The great astronomical question for anyone who isn't an astronomer is: "Are there intelligent beings on Mars? And if not, could human beings live there?"

Of course, people have wondered about life on all the planets. But for the past seventy-five years they have put their greatest hopes on Mars. For one thing, we know Mars could have an atmosphere for it is about half as big as the earth. For another, we know that

Mars is neither impossibly cold nor impossibly hot. And it has water in the form of snow and frost.

The excitement about Mars all started back in 1877. Every fifteen or seventeen years Mars comes within 35 million miles of the earth, and that year it was very close. This fact inspired the famous Italian astronomer, Schiaparelli, to make a really careful survey of its surface with his telescope. He discovered a remarkable thing that no one else had noticed.

Astronomers had been studying Mars with a telescope for over 200 years. They had seen certain dusky markings on it which were permanent. By watching these turn as the planet rotated, they had found that Mars has a day thirty-seven minutes longer than our day. They had also seen a large white spot grow at one of the poles, first one pole and then the other pole. Thinking it over, astronomers had decided that these were caps of snow, such as we have at our poles, and that they melted as the seasons changed on Mars. They thought the dusky markings were seas and the orange or rosy colored part of the surface was dry land.

Schiaparelli made a new discovery as he looked at Mars through a fine telescope night after night in the still air of Milan. He noticed a network of dusky streaks cutting across the "dry land" and connecting the "seas" with one another. He made a drawing of what he saw and called the dusky streaks *canali*, which in the Italian language can mean either *channels* or *canals.*

Nobody would have got excited if his word *canali* had been translated into English as *channels.* But calling the lines on Mars *canals* made all the difference in the world. Canals are something dug by human hands. To say there were canals on Mars was to imply that there were intelligent beings there who had dug them.

At once there was a sensation. "Canals? Then there must be people on Mars!" people said. "They probably have a big irrigation project up there. They are doubtless much more intelligent than we are. And why not? Really, it's not at all surprising. Mars is smaller and farther from the sun than we are. The planet must have cooled sooner than our earth. So very likely there has been life on Mars longer than here."

There was so much talk and excitement that the Lowell Observatory was set up in Arizona to study the planets and Mars in particular. Some people expected more signs of intelligent beings on Mars. A few talked about getting into communication with the Martians.

Others wondered why, if they were so much more advanced than we, the Martians hadn't been in touch with us. Maybe they were trying to, and we didn't understand their signals. Or maybe they were so advanced they didn't think we were worth getting in touch with.

What a letdown was in store! In time, astronomers found that the so-called "seas" were also crossed by canals. Obviously, then, the "seas" couldn't be seas; for how could water be crossed by canals? No, the dark areas must be the fertile parts of the planet, and the canals were long lines or valleys of growing plants. Anyone who watched the colors change would realize that, said observers. In the Martian "spring" and "summer," the fertile areas looked green. In the Martian "winter" they changed to brown, just as dying vegetation does. Moreover, the polar cap of snow grew smaller as summer came. Wasn't it obvious, they said, that the water ran from the ice near the North or South Pole and watered the vegetation?

It was a blow to be told that the canals weren't canals, that they weren't straight lines, that they weren't all connected in a network. It was painful to give up such exciting proof of intelligent beings on Mars. Some refused to believe the bad news. Some still refuse.

Yet everything leads us to believe that beings *like ourselves* couldn't possibly live there. Conditions on Mars are in many ways like those 62,000 feet above the surface of the earth. That's nearly twice as high as Mount Everest. Which means there just isn't enough air to breathe. In fact, conditions are such that even with plenty of oxygen piped into a space helmet a human being couldn't live. The air pressure would be lower than the water vapor and carbon dioxide in human lungs. And a strongly pressurized space suit would be clumsy. It is more probable that if anybody goes to Mars in the next 100 years he will either stay inside his space ship or travel around in some kind of small, air-conditioned tank.

If beings like ourselves couldn't live on Mars, it is proof that *nothing like* a human being is now living on that planet or ever has lived there. A great deal of nonsense has been written about life on Mars. But it is certain that nothing resembling human beings or any animals we know could possibly exist in the thin air and the severe cold. Only around noon does the temperature rise above freezing. And it is never higher than fifty or sixty degrees Fahrenheit. Besides, it even seems likely that there is no water on Mars. The snow and ice probably don't melt but simply turn into a trace of water vapor which spreads thinly through the planet's atmosphere.

What kind of plants, then, can be growing on Mars in a climate more bleak and unfriendly than anywhere on all the earth? We don't know. All we know is that something is growing there and is green. It may be a form of plant life even simpler than our mosses and lichens. If animals of any kind feed on this vegetation, we can only suppose that they are as small and simple as some of our insects.

But the fact that there is life at all on Mars is tremendously exciting. For what does it mean? It means that life is not an accident, that it didn't spring up by chance, that it is not a freak. It means that life comes into being wherever the conditions for life are possible. It gives us hope that life may exist somewhere else in the universe. Perhaps somewhere there may even be human beings like ourselves.

For astronomers there are wonderfully interesting things about Mars besides the question of life. There are, for instance, the two strange little moons that race around the planet. They are not at all like the earth's moon. They are so small they are really more like loose mountains tumbling around in space. Phobos, the inner moon, is only about ten miles across, and Deimos can hardly be more than five. This means they are hundreds of times smaller and millions of times lighter than our moon.

Phobos, being less than 4,000 miles from Mars, has to whiz around at a terrific pace and makes three trips in twenty-four hours. Deimos is 9,000 miles farther from the surface and takes thirty hours to make the circle. Looked at from Mars, the two moons must give an odd effect. To be sure, both travel in the same direction Mars travels around the sun. But Phobos would rise in the west and set in the east four and a half hours later. Deimos would rise in the east and stay visible in the sky for more than two days and two nights at a time. Before it set in the west, Deimos would be seen to go through all its phases from new moon to full moon twice.

Space-travel writers talk about observing Mars from one of these moons, but you might just as well be in free space as on one of them. Phobos and Deimos have so little gravitational pull that the slightest movement of any muscle would probably push the explorer away from these oversize rocks. Besides, their spinning might be quite an inconvenience.

9.

Baby Planets

As soon as astronomers started measuring distances, they noticed a strange thing—all the known planets but one were very regularly spaced. Each planet was roughly one and a half times as far from the sun as the one before. Jupiter was the exception. Between Mars and Jupiter there was a big gap.

"Why?" astronomers wondered. "Is it possible that this space is really empty?"

On the first of January, 1801, a Sicilian astronomer named Piazzi was looking through the telescope. He was making a catalog of the stars and knew the sky pretty well. So he was surprised to see a faint star where a few days before he hadn't seen any. The next night and the next he looked again. The faint star had moved regularly along. It was a planet, then!

Ceres was the first of the tiny planets which have been found racing around in the space between Mars and Jupiter. Pallas, Vesta and Juno followed. And since then a couple of thousand more minor planets, or asteroids as they are also called, have been discovered—some to be lost again. And plenty more asteroids are going to be found; for there are thousands more.

The asteroids are really very tiny planets. Ceres, the biggest, is only 480 miles across. Pallas is 300, Vesta 240. Not more than a dozen are over 100 miles across. Most are no more than a mile or two across. The little ones are not even round. They are just big mountains tumbling around in space. Put all together, those that have already been found don't weigh a thousandth part of the earth. They are such little things that they haven't a shred of an atmosphere among the lot; for the velocity of escape from the biggest is a third of a mile a second. They are such little things that except for Vesta, the brightest, they can't be seen with the naked eye. And through the telescope only a few of the biggest barely show a disk.

New ones are now discovered with a camera, for the astronomical camera catches what the eye cannot. If you expose a photographic plate to the sky for about half an hour, any minor planet there will make a streak on the plate. A star will show up as a dot. But an asteroid will leave a trail because it has been moving all the time. The camera is so much the best way to catch an asteroid that today nobody would try to spot a new one by means of a telescope. In the smaller sizes, hundreds and hundreds of asteroids have introduced themselves to us by photo.

The question used to be: "Why is there no planet between Mars and Jupiter?" Today the astronomers ask: "Why are there so many baby planets there? Are the asteroids bits of matter that never got together to form a planet? Or are they pieces of one that exploded long ago?"

Nobody knows. Perhaps we shall never know. We just quietly go on adding to the number of asteroids.

One of the most interesting things we know about the asteroids is that some of them come very close to us. One tiny one, which is really "out of place," comes closer than any planet. In May, 1932, it was only six and a half million miles from the earth. But it can come even closer—to within three million miles. Which is only twelve times farther off than the moon.

This need not startle anyone. There is not much danger of an asteroid bumping into us. Needless to say a five-mile minor planet hitting the earth would probably kill every human being on an entire continent. But the chance of such an accident happening is exceedingly slight. The earth can be said to be quite safe from such a calamity. It doesn't seem to have been hit that hard in the last couple of thousand million years.

10.

Galileo Looks at Jupiter

Beyond the asteroids, five times as far from the sun as we are, giant Jupiter spins along. Jupiter is so enormous that all the planets put together cannot make up its bulk. Jupiter is so big that 1,300 earths could be stuffed inside it.

The giant planet moves rather slowly. It takes twelve years to get around the sun. But for all its size, Jupiter turns on its axis faster than any other planet, and this makes it stick out in the middle. It sticks out to such an extent that it looks like a flattened ball.

Seen through a telescope that magnifies things sixty times, Jupiter is as big as the moon. And the first thing you notice is that it seems to be crossed by belts of blotches. These blotches change from week to week; so what can their meaning be? Just one. We are not looking at the solid surface of a rocky planet but at moving clouds floating above whatever surface Jupiter has. We are seeing zones of weird, dark clouds that are circling the planet above a covering of lighter colored clouds. Among these dark clouds astronomers have observed a big red spot 30,000 miles long and 7,000 miles wide. They have watched that spot for years. So it is clear that the dark bands around Jupiter are like no clouds we have on earth.

By studying the light reflected from Jupiter, we have found out that its clouds are a poisonous mixture of ammonia and methane, or marsh gas, floating in hydrogen and other gases. The gas layer is 10,000 miles thick! This means the pressure of that atmosphere is enormous. If ever a space ship gets through it without being crushed—which is quite unlikely—our explorers will not find out what Jupiter is like anyway. For they will land on a glacier that completely covers the planet. That ice is perhaps 10,000 miles thick. Naturally it's very cold on Jupiter. Our space-ship heroes will find the "air" even at the very top of the clouds colder than "dry ice." It is so cold that the ammonia must be either liquid or solid.

Uninviting though Jupiter is, almost anyone who is given a chance to handle a telescope is more than likely to turn it first on our moon and then on Jupiter. The four big moons of Jupiter are just about the most interesting things in the sky to watch through a telescope. Ever since Galileo discovered them revolving "like moths around a flame," they have been a show piece of the heavens.

He made this discovery in the very early days of the telescope, right after a Dutch spectacles maker had invented it. The news had quickly spread to Italy that things far off could be brought close by means of two pieces of glass—one convex and one concave—and a tube between them. On a visit to Venice, Galileo heard about the marvel and at once was fired with the ambition to make one for himself. As soon as he got back to Padua, he began tinkering with lenses meant for eyeglasses. And by the next day he had a telescope. His crude instrument brought things three times nearer! He could see things nine times larger! But Galileo wasn't satisfied. He had something in mind for which he needed more power. He set about improving his telescope. And eventually he had one that made things thirty times larger!

Originally nobody had thought of turning a telescope on the sky. The telescope was an instrument to be used in war, something to turn on the enemy to see what he was doing. People had, indeed, amused themselves by looking at church steeples and ships at sea, but it had never occurred to them to look at the heavens. First of all, Galileo turned his glass on the moon. Imagine his astonishment when he saw mountains more rugged than the earth's and pitted with craters! The face of the moon had always seemed so smooth and polished!

Sleep was forgotten. Night after night, while all but the watchmen of Padua were in their beds, Galileo glued his eye to his telescope. He turned it from the moon to the fixed stars and then to the planets. And now he realized that he had discovered more than his countryman who had crossed the Atlantic and found a continent. He had discovered worlds; for that is what the wandering lights he saw must be. The wanderers were worlds like the earth!

Feverish with excitement, he turned his telescope on the Milky Way. At once it came clear as a swarm of stars! Upon whatever part of it he directed his glass, straightway a vast crowd of stars presented itself to view. Some were large and extremely bright, but the number of small ones was so great that he found it impossible to determine how many there were.

One night some six or seven months after he had begun his observations, Galileo was sweeping the sky with his telescope when he came accidentally on Jupiter. For a moment he paused to look at it. And as he took in the image, he noticed three bright little stars near the planet. He was puzzled to find them arranged in a straight line. Two were on the east side of Jupiter, one was on the west.

The next night he turned his glass on the planet again. And to his amazement there were three little stars all on the west side of the planet! When two nights later he looked again and saw only two stars, both on the east side of Jupiter, he understood. The little stars weren't stars but moons, and there actually were four of them!

Nothing Galileo had seen in the heavens excited him so much. For in those moons of Jupiter he saw proof of a theory which only a few learned men believed, though Copernicus had proposed it long before. Nearly all thought that everything moved around the earth. Copernicus, however, believed all the planets went around the sun. Here were four moons moving around Jupiter. Perhaps this was a sort of model of the sun and its family—a miniature solar system!

Galileo wanted more evidence. Could Venus give it to him? Copernicus had said that as Venus moved around

A telescope on a tripod.

the sun it must pass through phases like the moon. He had foretold that sometimes it would show as a disk, sometimes as a crescent, sometimes as a quarter moon, and sometimes not at all.

In the greatest excitement, Galileo turned his telescope on Venus. And just as Copernicus had predicted, he saw Venus in the shape of a crescent.

This showed the planet did not shine by its own light. It must be reflecting the light of the sun. Venus showed only as much of herself as the sun lit up. And Mercury, being also between the earth and the sun, must do the same. To Galileo this meant there could no longer be any doubt that all the planets revolved around the sun. Some of the Greeks had believed it. Copernicus had believed it. The German, Kepler, believed it. The theory had never before been supported by the evidence of the senses. But now it was. One need only look through the telescope at Venus. One need only watch the moons of Jupiter.

All this still was not proof, and the telescopes were so poor no one got a really good look at anything. In those days many people held firmly to the idea that the earth was the center of the universe and that the sun and the stars had all been created for the sake of man.

The Church believed this strongly. Galileo was summoned to explain his position. He was threatened with torture if he didn't take back what he said about the earth moving. So Galileo took it all back and agreed not to teach the ideas of Copernicus. But as time went on, more and more people began to believe the earth was just one of a family of planets revolving around the sun.

No one can look at Jupiter and its moons and not see in them a model of the sun and its family. Actually it is a better model than Galileo thought. For besides its four big moons, Jupiter has eight little ones. Galileo didn't see them because they are really very small. Even we have seen but ten of the moons directly. Only photographs made with big telescopes reveal that there are twelve in all.

11.

A Planet With Rings

Jupiter with its moons is perhaps the most interesting object in the sky. But Saturn is certainly the most beautiful. Saturn is in a class by itself—no other planet can boast of rings.

Saturn is so light that it would float, for it weighs less than the same amount of water. And the reason for this is the layer of clouds which we consider part of Saturn. That layer of clouds is at least 16,000 miles deep! Then come thousands of miles of ice on top of a rock core. And like Jupiter's atmosphere, the atmosphere of Saturn is poisonous with ammonia and methane.

Saturn is the most flattened of all the planets, sticks out in the middle even more than Jupiter, and has almost as many moons—nine to be exact. But it is not these things that strike your eye looking through the telescope. It is the famous rings. The rings are really astonishing. They are 100,000 miles wider than the planet itself and look like a huge disk with a hole, into which the planet fits loosely. Through a four-inch telescope it is easy to see that there are really two flat rings with an empty space between. The space appears as a dark stripe. Through a really big telescope you can see that these two rings are also divided by faint stripes and that there is a faint, hazy ring between the inside edge of the inner ring and Saturn itself.

The impression you get is that the rings are perfectly solid. But we know they can't be. When a bright star is directly behind, we can see it through the rings—not so brightly shining but still there. Besides, we have found that the outermost parts don't travel as fast as the inner parts. In fact, each piece of the rings moves the way a moon would move at that distance from Saturn.

And, indeed, it turns out that each piece of the rings really is a tiny moon. The rings are made up of billions of strange little moonlets smaller than marbles, all going around as though the others weren't there. The moonlets are spread several yards apart all through the rings. There are so many that from nearly a thousand million miles away we see the moonlets all together as complete rings.

Where did all these moonlets come from? How did Saturn get its rings?

It may be that the moonlets are bits of matter that never got together to form a planet. But it is just as likely that they may be all that's left of a satellite that came too close to Saturn and paid for it with its life.

This isn't a fanciful guess. It has been worked out mathematically that a satellite *must* burst when it comes within a certain distance of a planet. The planet's mighty gravitational pull raises such tides on the moon that it breaks to pieces. Saturn's moon may have come into the danger zone. If so, it paid the penalty. Afterward the pieces tore around, bumped into one another, broke into smaller and smaller bits. And in accordance with the traffic laws of the sky, each tiny fragment found its bit of the road. Those that were traveling fastest took the inner lane, those traveling slowest took the outermost lane. And there were the rings.

Being out so far, Saturn moves pretty slowly—only one third as fast as the earth. Nearly thirty years pass before Saturn gets around the sun. And during that long "year" we see the rings from different angles because the planet is tilted over on one side. First we see the north side of the rings. A little more than seven years later we see them edge-on. After another seven years the south side of the rings is tilted toward the earth. Seven years more and we have them edge-on again and back to the way we saw them nearly thirty years before.

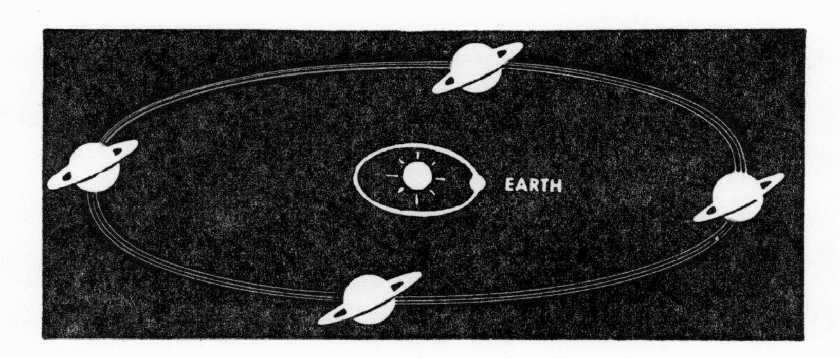

Because it tilts as it circles the earth, Saturn presents a different view of its rings every seven years.

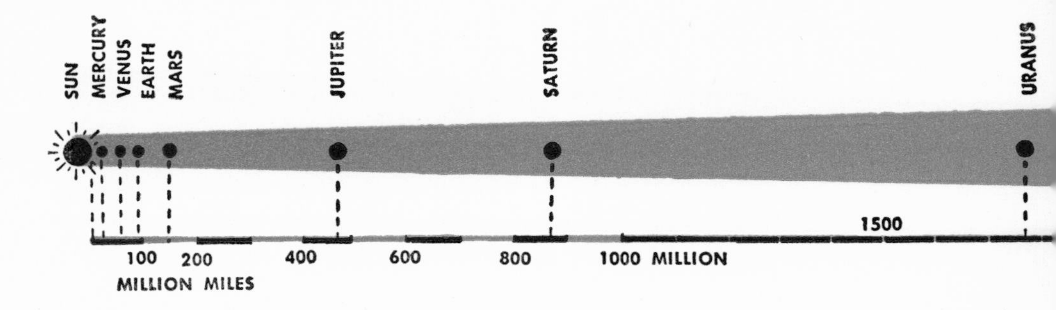

12.

Three Discoveries

Far out in space, a thousand million miles farther out than Saturn, is Uranus. And a thousand and more million miles beyond Uranus is its twin brother, Neptune. Out there where these planets travel, the sun's heat has become just warmth and is so feeble that the temperature is always colder than 300 below zero. It is so bitter cold on the planets that even the ammonia in their atmosphere has been frozen right out and only the persistent methane is left. As you would expect, Uranus and Neptune are well covered with ice below the methane clouds.

The twins aren't very interesting. They are much larger than the earth, but they aren't in the least spectacular even though Uranus can boast five moons and Neptune two. Uranus is so faint that a person must

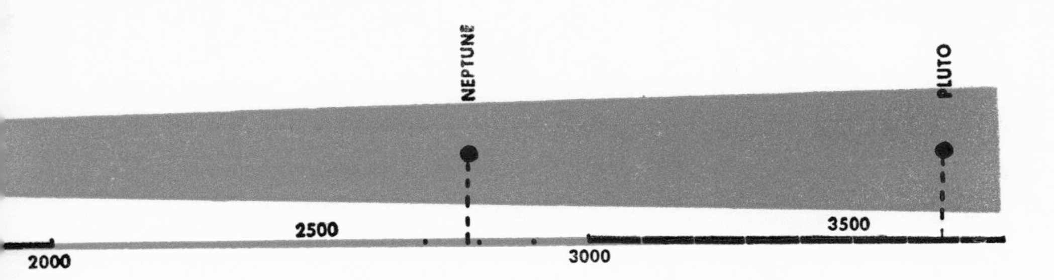

have very good eyesight to see it at all with the naked eye, while Neptune can be seen only with a telescope. And yet it is, after all, exciting to think that the sun's drawing power is so great that even at that immense distance it holds Uranus and Neptune close. Forever and forever the planets circle the sun that does so little for them. Uranus takes eighty-four years to get around, Neptune almost twice as long.

The two planets are newcomers to the sun's family as we know it, and seeing how faint they are, it isn't to be wondered at. Uranus was just an accidental find. It was discovered in 1781 by William Herschel, an amateur. He had built his own telescope and was going over the wonders it revealed to him one by one. One night Herschel saw a star that looked different. He was a musician, not a trained astronomer, but he realized at once this couldn't be a star because it showed a disk. This was so far out from the sun that it never occurred to him his star might be a planet. He thought it was a comet perhaps. And for a while all the astronomers to whom he pointed it out agreed. They thought it was a comet without a tail. But, studying the way Uranus moved, they finally decided it was a planet, even though 'way off there.

It was while they were studying Uranus that Neptune came into the picture. Uranus didn't behave the way the astronomers thought it should. It seemed to vary from the usual path. Why? Was there still another planet out in space? Was that planet pulling Uranus off the path on which, according to Newton's law, it should have stayed?

In the 1840's a young student at Cambridge University in England was fascinated with these questions about Uranus. "As soon as I graduate," Adams said to himself, "I'm going to put all my mind on it." And he did. He worked out the problem of Uranus by mathematics. In two years' time he figured out exactly what part of the sky a planet would have to be in to make Uranus go off the road that way.

An astronomer at Cambridge started looking. He looked for the planet for months. He measured the position of 3,000 stars in the region Adams indicated, to see if one of them would show by "wandering" that it was a planet. He was about to make a chart of his stars when news came that an astronomer in Berlin had found the planet.

A young Frenchman named Leverrier had had exactly the same idea as Adams. Like Adams he had worked the problem out by mathematics. And he had arrived at the same answer. He, too, had been in touch with an astronomer. But the German observer had an advantage over the English one. He already had a chart of the stars for the exact region of the sky which Leverrier had asked to be searched. All the German astronomer had to do was look through the telescope and see if something that didn't show on the map was in that part of the sky. And sure enough there was—Neptune. It had taken him just one night to find it.

Finding Neptune explained why Uranus behaved the way it did. But only to an extent. Neptune wasn't the whole explanation. Was there still another planet in the family of the sun?

Years later Percival Lowell, the same Lowell after whom the Lowell Observatory in Arizona was named, started to work on the problem. The figures he had to work with weren't as good as in the case of Neptune. Nevertheless, he went ahead and calculated in

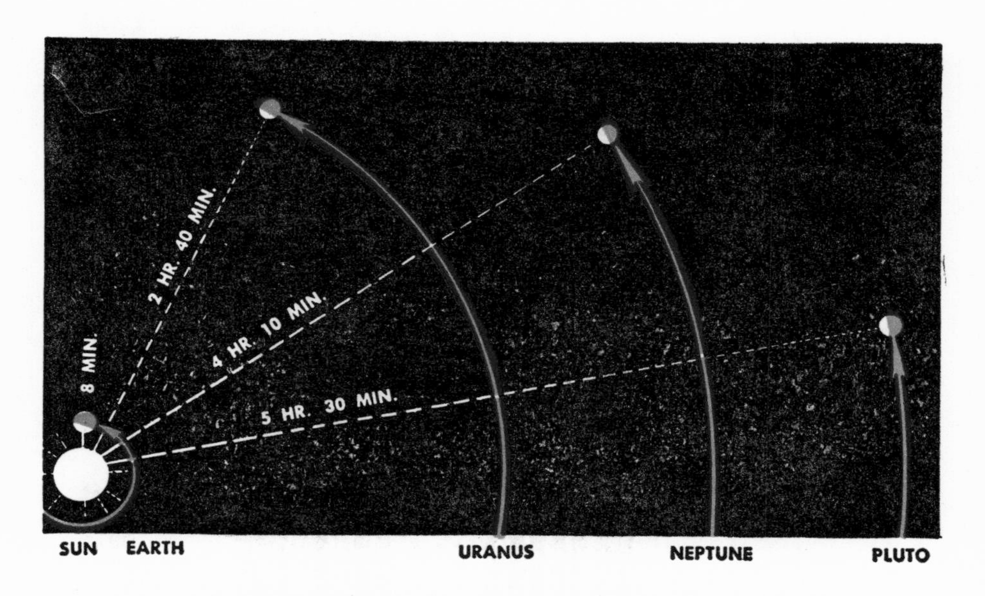

Pluto is so far away that it takes 5½ hours for the sun's light to reach it.

what part of the sky the suspected planet should be looked for. He predicted its path and even worked out how much the planet ought to weigh.

Fourteen years after Lowell's death, an astronomer at Lowell Observatory found Pluto. He found it by taking two photographs several days apart of likely regions in the sky. By comparing each set of two, he could tell if any change had taken place. And one day he did see a change. One little point of light had moved —as only a "wanderer" would. It was another planet!

The little point of light turned out to be only one-ninth as large as predicted. Pluto proved to be so small, indeed, that the effect it has on Uranus can't possibly be noticed. If Lowell had started out knowing the size of Pluto—which weighs as much as the earth—and its place in the sky, he could never have worked out from that the way Uranus wobbles. So finding Pluto in the very place Lowell predicted can only be looked on as a coincidence and a wonderful piece of luck. For there are twenty million stars in the sky as bright as Pluto. Which is to say that Pluto was as well hidden as a needle in a haystack. If Lowell, by his wrong calculation, hadn't chanced to direct astronomers to the particular piece of sky where Pluto really happened to be, the ninth planet would probably never have been found.

Little Pluto is a cold world—400° below zero Fahrenheit. The sun shines on it only $\frac{1}{1500}$ as brightly as it does on us, for Pluto is thirty-nine times farther from the sun than the earth—so far away that a Pluto year is equal to 224 of ours. Perhaps in the far-off reaches of the solar system there are other planets still colder, still less habitable. If there are, they must be very faint and far away. We can hardly expect to find them except by lucky chance.

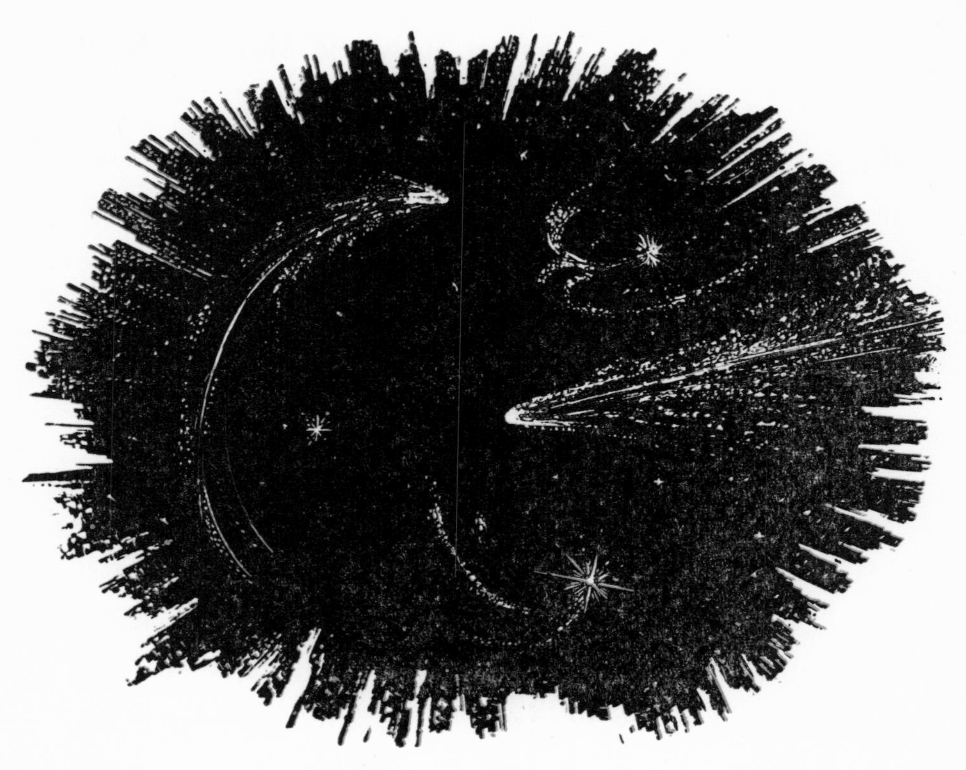

13.

Hairy Stars and Shooting Stars

In olden days whenever anything extraordinary happened in the sky, people thought it had a special meaning for mankind. A new very bright star would generally spell something good. An eclipse might bode good or ill and needed very careful interpreting. But a comet was always supposed to be bad. It foretold death, disease and destruction.

Actually, comets aren't extraordinary events. Only

the spectacular ones are rare. Though you can't see them with the naked eye, there are thousands of comets around. Through the telescope they look like little bright bits of cloud lacking the tails which gave comets their name of *hairy stars*.

Some of the hairy stars belong to our solar system and never leave it; others are visitors from a region far beyond the sun. Some comets come back time and time again. We know exactly when to expect them. Halley's Comet, for instance, came in 1910 and will surely be back again in 1986. We have records—with some gaps—back to 170 B.C. They show how this comet has returned every seventy-six years. Other comets come oftener, while some come so seldom that we don't know whether they have been here more than once.

But whether they visit us often or seldom, they all travel around the sun. Their path is generally a very flat ellipse. They loop around in such a way that they rush close to the sun, even closer than Mercury does, and then sail slowly so far out that they are much too faint to be seen. When they are near the sun, they move from one constellation to the next in a matter of days. Sometimes we can see the same comet every night for a week.

What are these startling heavenly objects that used to terrify people into thinking doom was coming?

Comets are strange mixtures. Their heads are swarms of mile-big lumps of rock and metal and ice and solidified gases. Their tails are gases and dust which the sun's rays seem to brush away from the head. Far out in space a comet has no tail. The tail appears only when the comet approaches the sun and the rays start to work on it. This tail streams out like smoke behind the comet and gets longer and longer as the comet nears the sun. When the comet has looped around and is going off again, the tail goes ahead. Always the tail points away from the sun.

Is a comet large?

Yes and no. Certainly, it covers a great deal of space. The tail of a comet sometimes streams out for 50 or 100 million miles. But for its size, a comet weighs remarkably little. The earth probably weighs a million times more than all the stuff making up a big comet. Yet we know that a comet may weigh thousands of millions of tons.

The reason a comet weighs so little is that the particles of which it is made are very far apart. There is less matter in a cubic mile of its tail than in a cubic

The tail of a comet may stream out for millions of miles.

inch of the air in a room. The head is not compact either. It is made up of big pieces that may weigh as much as many tons, little pieces the size of marbles, and specks of dust. There are probably only a few chunks in every cubic mile of comet head.

If you have seen a meteorite exhibited in a museum, you know what a piece of a comet's head looks like. For meteorites—at least a great many of them—are bits of gravel from a worn-out comet. We know that many a comet that once used to visit us has broken up as its ice was boiled away by the sun. The rocks and metal that made up the head scattered along the path the comet used to follow. They kept right on going in a great swarm. They are still going around.

On a clear August night you can probably see a couple of dozen meteors or shooting stars. The streaks of light come from the violent burning of the speck of rock as it runs into our atmosphere at more than 30,000 miles an hour. They are exciting and beautiful things to watch; they make you think of fireworks. The reason we see them in August is because that is one of the times the earth crosses a path which a comet once followed and where its pieces still continue to travel. We call such a path a *meteor track*.

But it's not only in August that you can see meteors. You can spot one or two or more almost any night. Every day some thousand million meteors enter our atmosphere. Almost all of them are smaller than a pea. We see only a few of them because they are so small and make such a tiny flare as they heat up and burn.

Very seldom does a meteor get to within forty miles of us, and still more rarely does one manage to survive the trip through our atmosphere and strike the earth. When one does, we call it a meteorite. As a rule, meteorites are quite small, but some have been found that weigh many tons.

Once in a great while a meteor is so big and bright that it can be seen in broad daylight. Such a "rock from space" flames across the skies of several states. Often it explodes in the air and drops meteorite stones or bits of iron over hundreds of acres of land. In the last 100,000 years only a few meteors have hit the earth. One made the huge Meteor Crater in Arizona. Another, about 10,000 years ago, blasted a hole two miles wide in northern Canada. But such collisions are very rare.

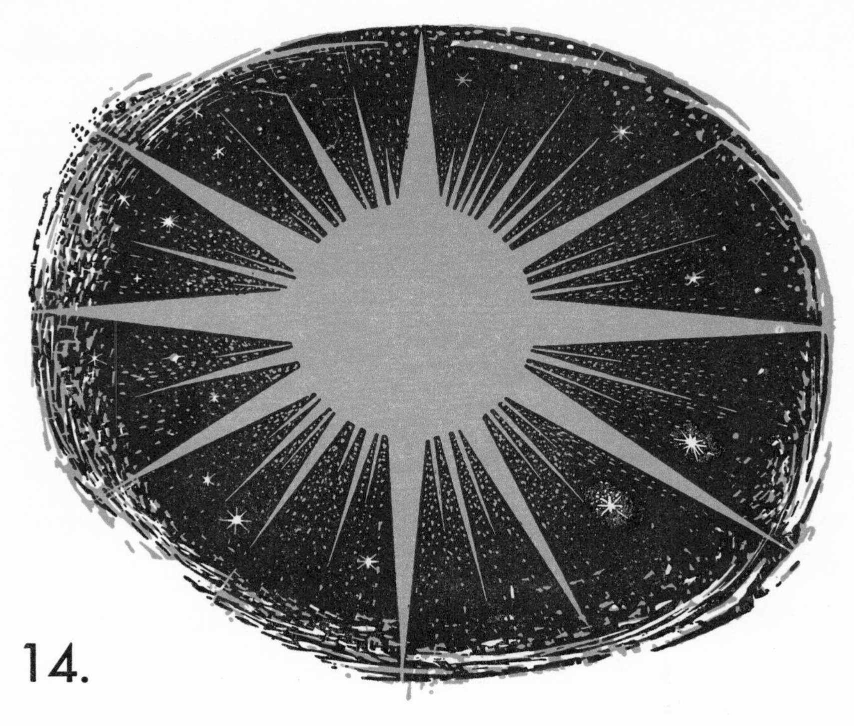

14.

The Stars Are Many and Far Away

The summer sun beats down on us—it is ninety degrees in the shade. We long for the beach, we long for rain, we long for the day to pass. Night comes, and still it is unbearably hot. We go out of the stuffy house, lie down on the grass, look up—and there are the stars unconcernedly winking at us.

"Is it really possible," we think, "that those little points of light are suns like our sun? Can they really be as big and hot?"

It is hard to believe. It seems impossible that the sun is a star and the stars are suns. And yet it is so. The only real difference between the sun and the stars is distance. If the sun were moved out to where the nearest star is, our sun would be just a bright point in the sky. If the nearest star were put in place of the sun, the star's rays would light and warm the earth just as nicely as the sun's rays do now. And our lives would go on just the same.

Distance is everything. Distance makes all the difference between the glare of the sun and the glint of the stars. But it is hard to understand such vast distance. When we say the nearest star is twenty-five million million miles away, it makes no impression on us.

And it is no better when we think of any freak number—like the number of times a watch would tick in a thousand years. The number of ticks is still too small to compare to the number of miles we are from the stars. If every tick were a mile, a watch would have to run for a million years to tick out the distance to some of the brightest stars.

No, when we talk about the stars we have to give up measuring in miles. It makes less sense than measuring around the earth in inches. Instead of miles our measuring stick can be the speed of light. When speaking of the distance to a star, we will not say, "How many miles is it?" Instead, we will say, "How long does it take light to travel that far?"

In the beginning of this book, you will remember we said light travels faster than anything else. It goes 186,000 miles a second. We said that it takes light more than four years to travel from the nearest star to us. The nearest star, then, is over four light years away. The light we see winking up there now started out on its journey more than four years ago and has just reached our eye.

Four light years has more meaning than 25 million million miles, but a scale model will show even better what that distance means. Let a grapefruit represent the sun. To be in scale, the earth would be represented by a bead $\frac{1}{16}$ of an inch across, spinning fifty feet away. Let another grapefruit represent our nearest star. Where shall we set it? A mile away? Ten?

Think again. That grapefruit would have to be set 2,600 miles away! If we put our grapefruit sun in New York City, our grapefruit star would be in Reno, Nevada!

That's how far we are from the nearest star. That's

what four light years means. The wonder is not that the stars seem so small but that we see them at all. The wonder is that we see so many.

About five thousand stars in all the sky around the solar system can be seen with the naked eye. To be sure, nobody can see that many at one time. For half the stars are below the horizon, and the fainter ones near the horizon are dimmed by the air. On a clear night in the summer when the Big Dipper is almost overhead, not everyone will be able to see half a dozen stars inside the Big Dipper's bowl. And as there are no more than 600 stars this bright or brighter in the sky at the same time, we cannot see very many in any one area or constellation. Two thousand is about the limit anyone can see at one time under the best conditions.

More than a hundred years before the birth of Christ, a Greek astronomer named Hipparchus made the first catalog of the stars. He had 1,080 stars in it. And he labeled each one according to its brightness. He divided the stars into six classes. The brightest he called stars of the *first magnitude*. The next brightest he called stars of the *second magnitude*. And so on down to stars of the *sixth magnitude*. No star fainter than these could be seen with the naked eye. Naturally, Hipparchus must have supposed that's all there were.

Not until Galileo turned his telescope on the stars, did we learn of less bright stars. Now, with a pair of simple binoculars, we can count twenty times as many stars as we can with our eyes alone. Through a large telescope we can count many times more again. And

Hipparchus made the first catalog of the stars.

an astronomical camera can see even more. The 200-inch telescope at the Palomar Observatory in California photographs stars of the twenty-first magnitude—a million times too faint for you to see.

How many stars are there, then, altogether?

We don't know. We know that with our largest telescope several thousand million stars could be photographed. But we know also that when we have developed a stronger telescope we have seen a myriad new stars. We can only conclude that there must be thousands of millions more beyond those we can see now. It staggers the imagination to think how many stars there are.

Astronomers try to think of ways to bring home to people the number of the stars. One says, "There are more stars in the sky than there are grains of sand on all the beaches of the world." Another says, "There are more stars in the sky than there are letters in a million books." It is bewildering.

And it is just as staggering to think of distances. For even the nearest stars are so far away that we never see them except as points of light. We wouldn't see even those if the stars weren't so hot, or so big, or both.

When Hipparchus made his catalog of the stars, he

thought they were "fixed" to a sphere and were all equally far away. So, naturally, he believed their magnitude was their real brightness. But we know that one star only *seems* to be brighter than another. Whether or not it *really* is brighter depends chiefly on how hot it is and how far away it is.

How do we know how far away a star is?

It is easy to measure how far away the moon and the planets and the sun are. You can find those distances the same way a surveyor does when he wants to find the distance to some object on the earth. But when it comes to the stars, there is trouble. You can't use ordinary range-finding methods. The stars are too far away.

Not until 1838 did anyone measure the distance to a star. At that time people still thought that the brightest stars were the nearest stars. So whoever thought about measuring how far it was to a star generally concerned himself with the *bright* stars. But an astronomer named Bessel had a different idea. He said to himself, "The nearest stars are not necessarily the ones that are brightest. It is more likely that the nearest stars are those which seem to move the fastest. For isn't it the same with stars as with flying birds? When we see two birds flying, one near and the other far off, the one near us seems to fly faster. It seems so even when the far-off bird is flying faster."

Now, of course, most of the stars move so slowly that in a lifetime we can't notice the difference in their positions. But Bessel knew one star that moved pretty fast. It was called #61 in the constellation of the Swan and was the fastest moving star known at that time. It moved so fast that in 300 years it would cover a space as big as the full moon appears to be. Bessel decided he would measure how much this "fast-moving" star would "shift" its position in six months' time. He would sight exactly where it was with respect to another star. And then, six months later, when the earth had moved all the way to the other side of its track around the sun and was 186 million miles away, he would take another look from the new position.

You will understand Bessel's plan better if you try a simple experiment. Hold your finger out in front of you, and look at it with your right eye. Now close it and look with the left eye. Your finger seems to shift to the right. That's because your eyes are about two and a half inches apart. Your second look is from two and a half inches away.

Now Bessel, with his telescope eye, intended to take

his second look from a distance 186 million miles away. He expected that his star, even though it was so far off, would shift a little.

And it did! It moved just a tiny, tiny bit—as much as the width of a quarter held up at a distance six miles away. From this tiny "shift" he worked out that his star was over half a million times as far away as the sun, or about a million million miles away from us.

Since Bessel measured that first star, astronomers have measured the distance to thousands of stars. Nowadays, however, they don't have to do what he did. All that's necessary is to measure the shift of a star on photographs taken six months apart. Star distances as far as 100 light years away can be measured this way.

What have astronomers learned from their measurements? What do they know about the distances of the stars?

Amazing things. We have found that all but a very few stars are infinitely farther away than #61 in the constellation of the Swan. Though the nearest star is half that far, altogether *only seven stars besides the sun are within ten light years*, or sixty million million miles of us. Some stars are hundreds, and thousands, and millions of light years away. When we look at the stars, we see the past. For there are stars so far away that their light started on its way to us before the American Revolution was fought. There are stars so far away that the light we see streaming from them now left them before Rome was founded. There are stars whose light started on its way to us when dinosaurs roamed our country.

If you want to look back into history, there is no easier way than to lift your eyes to the stars.

15.

How Big? How Bright? How Fast?

You may be sure astronomers didn't stop with measuring the distances to the stars. Next they determined brightness. When they knew both, they could easily figure out how much light a star *really* gave. And that was a great help in understanding the stars.

They found out that of the seven "nearby" stars, Alpha Centauri, the nearest of all, is most like our sun. It is the same in color and temperature and gives off the same amount of light.

They discovered that Sirius, another of the "nearby" stars, has good reason to look the brightest star in the heavens. You have probably had the constellation

Orion, the Mighty Hunter, pointed out to you in the winter sky. He is beside the Milky Way. Orion's belt is three bright stars in a row. Down below his right foot is his dog, and that's where Sirius is. Well, Sirius is so bright in part because it is so near, but in part because it is so hot. It is bluer in color and hotter than the sun. So, although it isn't much bigger, it gives off thirty times as much light and heat.

Astronomers went right on and learned the color and brightness of a great many stars up to 100 light years away and even beyond. And from what they know of these, they can guess what even the most distant stars are like. For example, they know that stars shining with a blue light are very hot. If a star is so hot that it is "blue" hot and it still doesn't look bright in the telescope, they know it must be a long way off indeed. It must be so because every "blue" star they have studied shines far more brilliantly than the sun. Some of the "blue" stars are 10,000 times brighter than the sun. The "red" stars, on the other hand, are cooler. Yet, if they are big enough, they may give off even more heat than the blue stars.

Now, the stars had been just *stars* for so long it was quite a surprise to learn they are so different from one another. Astronomers found stars that are giants and stars that are dwarfs, stars that are exceedingly hot, and stars that in comparison are coolish or cool. It was confusing at first. But little by little, as astronomers studied and measured and compared, the character of the sky as a whole came clear.

We know now that the very brilliant stars are the exceptions. There aren't very many stars 10,000 times brighter than the sun. For every star as bright as that there are 100,000 like the sun. Still, for every star brighter than the sun there are fifteen or more that are fainter. Most stars fall into a "normal" group to which the sun also belongs. It is a good sample star—not one that would be passed over in a crowd, yet not one that would stand out surprisingly.

Compared with these "normal" stars, these "rank and file" stars, the giants are enormous. Some are a hundred times as big as the sun. Some of the red stars are so big that if one were put where the sun is, it would reach out to where the earth is and swallow it. Instead of being 93 million miles away from the sun, we would be right inside it.

And the dwarfs, of which there are several different kinds, are enormously smaller than the sun. The white

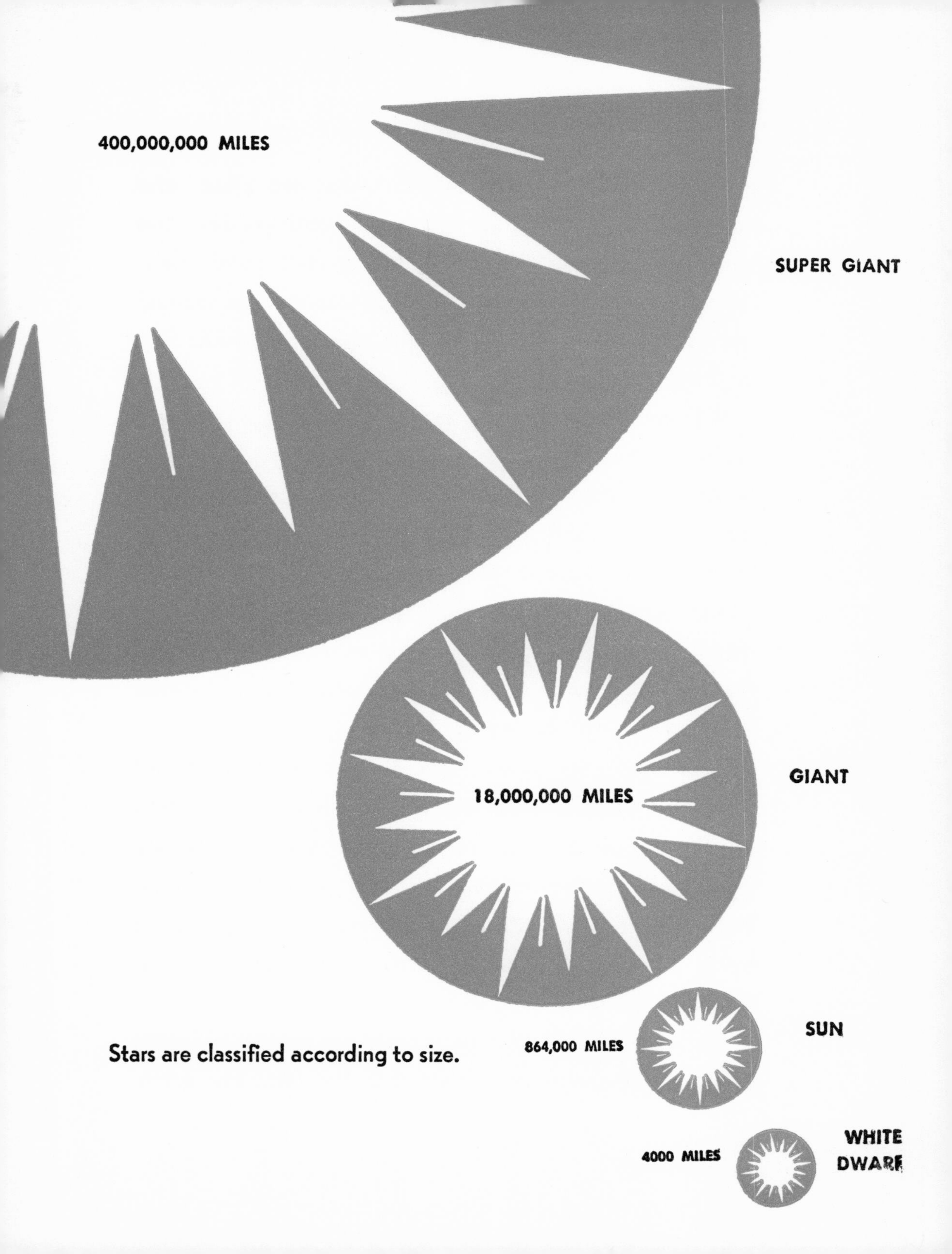

Stars are classified according to size.

dwarfs are the strangest stars of all. They are such small squeezed-up things that they are no bigger than a planet and can be seen only with the largest telescope. Yet a typical white dwarf weighs as much as the sun. Think how tight the "star stuff" must be packed for this to be true! It is packed so tight that a piece of white dwarf weighs 6,000 times as much as an equally big piece of iron. One quart of white dwarf would weigh fifty tons! Fantastic as that sounds, there are stars made of even heavier stuff.

Because we take our sun to be a good sample star, you will guess that other stars keep on shining for the same reason the sun does. And your guess will be right. Practically all of them do. Practically all the stars feed on themselves. Deep inside their core they are turning hydrogen into helium.

But here is the interesting thing—not all the stars are using up their hydrogen at the same rate. Where the stars are *no bigger* than our sun, they are just as economical and in no more danger of using up their hydrogen in a hurry than our sun is. But when it comes to the big stars, the story is different. The big stars are spendthrifts; they are using up their hydrogen fast. And the bigger a star is, the more of a spendthrift it is.

A star twice as big as the sun is using up its hydrogen twelve times as fast. A star ten times as big is using it up 1,000 times as fast. And a star 100 times as big is using up its hydrogen a million times as fast. Such a star, you can see, is going to be in trouble before long. It is bound to use up its hydrogen. Some stars have already done this so that now the only way they can keep on shining is by shrinking. That's how the white dwarfs got that way. They used up their hydrogen and had to shrink to stay hot and bright.

Well, there the stars are—thousands of millions of them. Are they doing anything besides shining?

Yes. The stars are moving. The moon goes around the earth, the earth goes around the sun, and the sun goes rapidly through space. It moves in a great stream of star traffic. Some of the stars are going our way around a great circular track in the Milky Way. Others are cutting right across our path. But they all belong to our system of stars—the Milky Way System, our galaxy. All the stars we can see with the naked eye belong to our galaxy.

You will remember that star #61 in the constellation of the Swan travels so fast that in 300 years it moves the seeming width of the moon. But what is the real speed of the stars? How fast is the star traffic in our galaxy actually moving?

The stars are moving at 10,000 to 100,000 miles an hour. Our sun overtakes a good many of the stars on our track because we are making 40,000 miles an hour.

We can't see far ahead as we move along with the sun. We can't see to the other side of the track. There is dust that obscures our road. For all that, we know where we are headed. We are moving in the direction of the constellation Cygnus the Swan. But have no fear. There isn't going to be a smash-up. We have lots and lots of room to get by. The traffic lanes of the sky are immensely wide. Stars are, in general, 50 million times as far apart as they are big. They are practically lost in space.

Remember? When we put our grapefruit sun in New York, we had to put the nearest grapefruit star in Reno, Nevada. That's how much space there is between the stars. So don't think of our track in the Milky Way as being crowded. Not one star in a thousand million ever hits another star. Star traffic is almost absolutely safe.

16.

Companions in the Sky

We speed along the mighty track within the Milky Way—yet we don't feel a thing. We sense the motion no more than our turning and spinning around the sun. Calmly, we look around us at the nearest travelers in the wide lanes of the sky. We turn our telescope this way and that. And all of a sudden we give a start—what we took to be a single point of light turns out to be two separate stars very close together.

"But you said that stars are very far apart!" I hear you exclaim. "You said there's so much space they practically never run into each other!"

That's right. What we see isn't a traffic accident about to take place. This pair of stars has always been close together. They are twins, they grew up together. They move around each other and are proceeding in company. There are lots of stars like that. Perhaps about half of all stars are double. Of the eight stars nearest to us, five have companions, and one of the five has two. The sun, which travels alone, is the exception rather than the rule.

Even without binoculars you can see some of the pairs for yourself. Look up at the bend of the handle

There are twin stars at the bend of the Big Dipper's handle.

of the Big Dipper. That star has a fainter star above it. If you have very good eyesight, you can spot other double stars. But a telescope brings thousands within your reach. You will see double stars that are exactly like each other—they seem like identical twins. And you will see many more that aren't at all alike.

Sirius, the Dog Star, for example, has a very different twin. Astronomers, who like to have their joke, call this twin the "Pup." The "Pup" is a very dim star and seems all the dimmer because Sirius is so bright. The "Pup" is as heavy as the sun and even hotter at the surface. But it is only one-fiftieth as bright as the sun and not much more than that in size. In fact, it is one of those spendthrift stars that spent all its hydrogen very fast and is now getting on as best it can by shrinking. It is a white dwarf. It has shrunk so much that a cube of it one inch big would weigh a ton.

To the astronomer double stars aren't just something to admire. He could hardly manage without them. For the weight of a star is its most important property—how bright it is depends largely on that—and double stars are the only ones that can be weighed. Watching the two companion stars move around each other, an astronomer can figure out just how big a pull they must exert in order to stay that close together. And from the pull he can get the weight.

Considering how many different kinds of stars there are, what astronomers have found out about weight is really quite surprising. The differences in weight are nothing like the differences in brightness. Not many stars are more than ten times as heavy as the sun. Not many stars weigh less than a fifth as much.

Now you must not suppose that companion stars are always very near each other. Some companions are so far apart that it takes them hundreds of years or even more to go around each other. But even without knowing that, you would appreciate that in far-off double stars the companions have to be thousands of millions of miles apart to show as double stars at all. You've had experience with distance—you know how railroad tracks seem to come together in the distance. Probably there are many double stars so far off that they show as one even through the biggest telescopes.

On the other hand, there are many pairs in which the companions are quite close together. Some are so close that they roll around each other in days instead of years. Some are so close they whip around one another in a few hours. Such close double stars, like the very far-off ones, can never be "seen" as anything but one star. And yet astronomers do manage to observe the close twins separately.

For example, when two stars revolve so close to each other that they nearly touch, one star will seem to cover part of the other most of the time. In other words, one star "eclipses" the other—or part of it—every time it comes between us and the other star.

Now, of course, we never see a star as a disk because

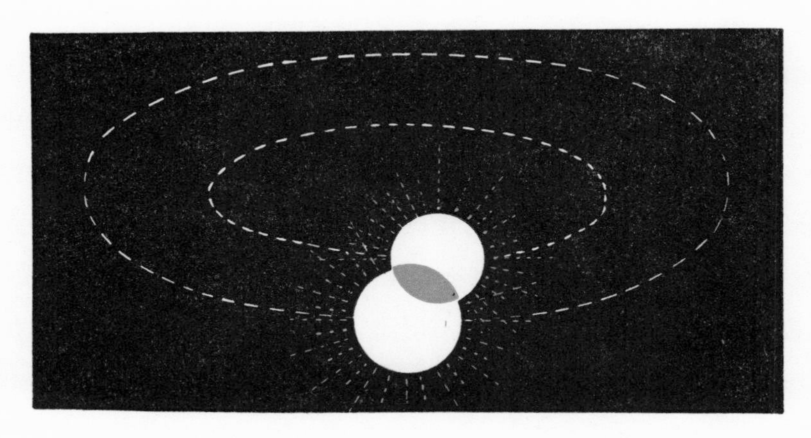

Sometimes one companion star "eclipses" the other.

every star except the sun is too far away. So what we see when one star eclipses another is just a change in their combined light. The light grows dimmer. The astronomer measures the brightness—as often as every three minutes for some pairs of stars. Then, on a piece of paper, he draws a line that "dips" the way the light "dips" when one star moves over in front of the other.

It is quite amazing how much an astronomer can get out of a curvy line like that after doing a lot of complicated figuring. Once he knows the distance of the stars and has analyzed the light, he can get the size of each one of the stars in miles. He can tell how many tons each one weighs. He can tell how hot each one is, how bright on an average a square foot of their surfaces is, how fast they are traveling, and even how much they pull each other out of shape.

It is somehow comforting to know that the stars aren't scattered over the sky just at random, helter-skelter, any which way. People like to see pattern, and double stars are a bit of pattern.

But they aren't the only bit of pattern. Some double stars turn out to be triple, or even two sets of pairs, or three sets. And besides these, there are larger clusters—whole groups of stars that travel in company. There are clusters made up of hundreds and even thousands of stars.

One brilliant little group is called the Pleiades. It forms a sort of "Baby Dipper" in the constellation Taurus, the Bull. When you look at the Pleiades on a clear winter night, you can easily pick out the six brightest stars. Quite a few people are able to see nine or ten stars if there are no street lights and if their eyes are adjusted to the darkness. But with any kind of binoculars you can see fifty or more stars right in the same area.

The Pleiades form part of the constellation Taurus, the Bull.

Several hundred still fainter stars can be seen with the telescope.

Such "open clusters" of stars are found all along the Milky Way all over the sky. You can find some of them for yourself—like the Beehive Cluster in the constellation of the Crab. Or there's the famous Double Cluster in the north, between Perseus and Cassiopeia. It can be seen most of the night all through the year. But don't look for any pattern in the clusters—they are just bunched-up stars.

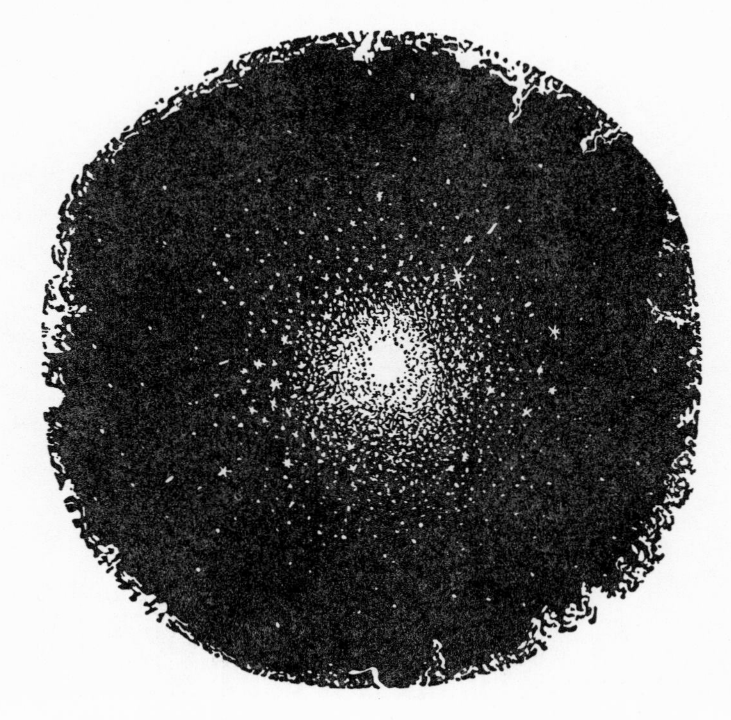

Globular clusters are like mammoth balls of stars.

They've always been bunched-up that way. They are families that spend their lives together and travel the sky lanes in a group.

You must think that families composed of hundreds or thousands of members are pretty large. Yet there are star clusters of another sort that are even larger. We call them *globular clusters* because they are like mammoth balls of stars. In the Northern Hemisphere where we live we can see only one such cluster with the naked eye—in the constellation Hercules. But altogether, about a hundred globular clusters are known. In each cluster there are hundreds of thousands of stars. About 100,000 of them are brighter than the sun, while the brightest are 300 times brighter.

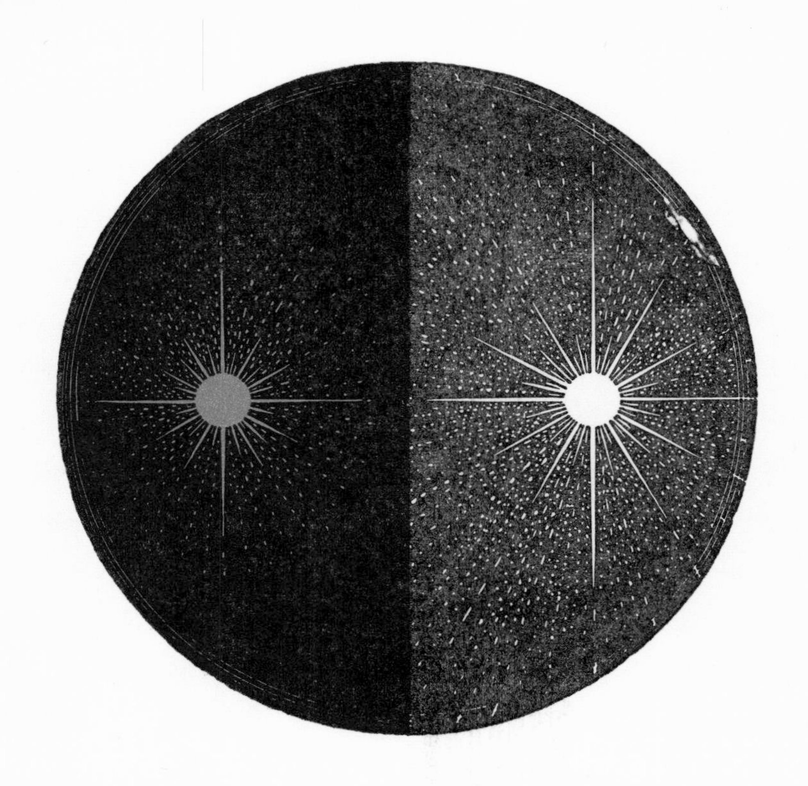

17.

Stars That Vary Their Light

Early on a winter morning in the year 1901, an astronomer in Edinburgh, Scotland, was out looking at the stars. Dr. Anderson was just an amateur, but he knew his stars. So when his eye lit on a certain moderately bright star in the constellation Perseus, his heart gave a bound. The star was new! There had been no star in that place before!

Dr. Anderson lost no time getting in touch with an observatory, and in an hour the news was on the wires. Every astronomer who could get to a telescope jumped to it. All over the world eyes turned on the new star in Perseus. For the most exciting thing that ever happens in the sky was happening, and nobody wanted to miss the "big show."

The star grew rapidly brighter. By the following night it was so bright that it was almost the brightest star in the sky. But on the next night after that it had already started to fade. Slowly it grew dimmer and dimmer. A year later you could just barely see it with the naked eye.

What happened? Why all the excitement? Had a new star actually been born?

At that time astronomers didn't really know what had happened. All they knew was that the new star in Perseus wasn't actually new—it had been there all the time but shining so faintly that nobody could see it with the naked eye. They had watched the dim star suddenly grow very bright, then fade. And the same sort of thing, they knew, had happened a number of times before. Records showed that through the centuries several such new stars had been seen. They had been called *new stars* or *novae* because in the days before telescopes astronomers had really thought that a new star had been born. But not for 300 years had a nova so bright as this been seen. Had some terrible accident occurred in the sky? Had two stars run into each other?

The last fifty years have solved the puzzle of new stars and super-new stars—ordinary novae and supernovae. We now know they have nothing to do with traffic accidents in the sky. As one astronomer put it, the stars are so far apart that there is less chance of a collision between two stars than between two rowboats that have the whole Pacific Ocean to themselves. New stars are oversize stars in trouble with nobody but themselves.

You remember that the bigger a star is, the faster it uses up its hydrogen? Well, a nova is one of these spendthrift giants that has got to the end of its hydrogen. It used up its resources and had to shrink. It shrank and shrank, and the more it shrank, the faster it had to rotate. Finally it got going so fast that it started to break up. It shot off its whole outer atmosphere and sent it racing out into space like a brilliant bubble.

That is what makes a star appear 10,000 times brighter than before. At the time of the explosion, its much hotter

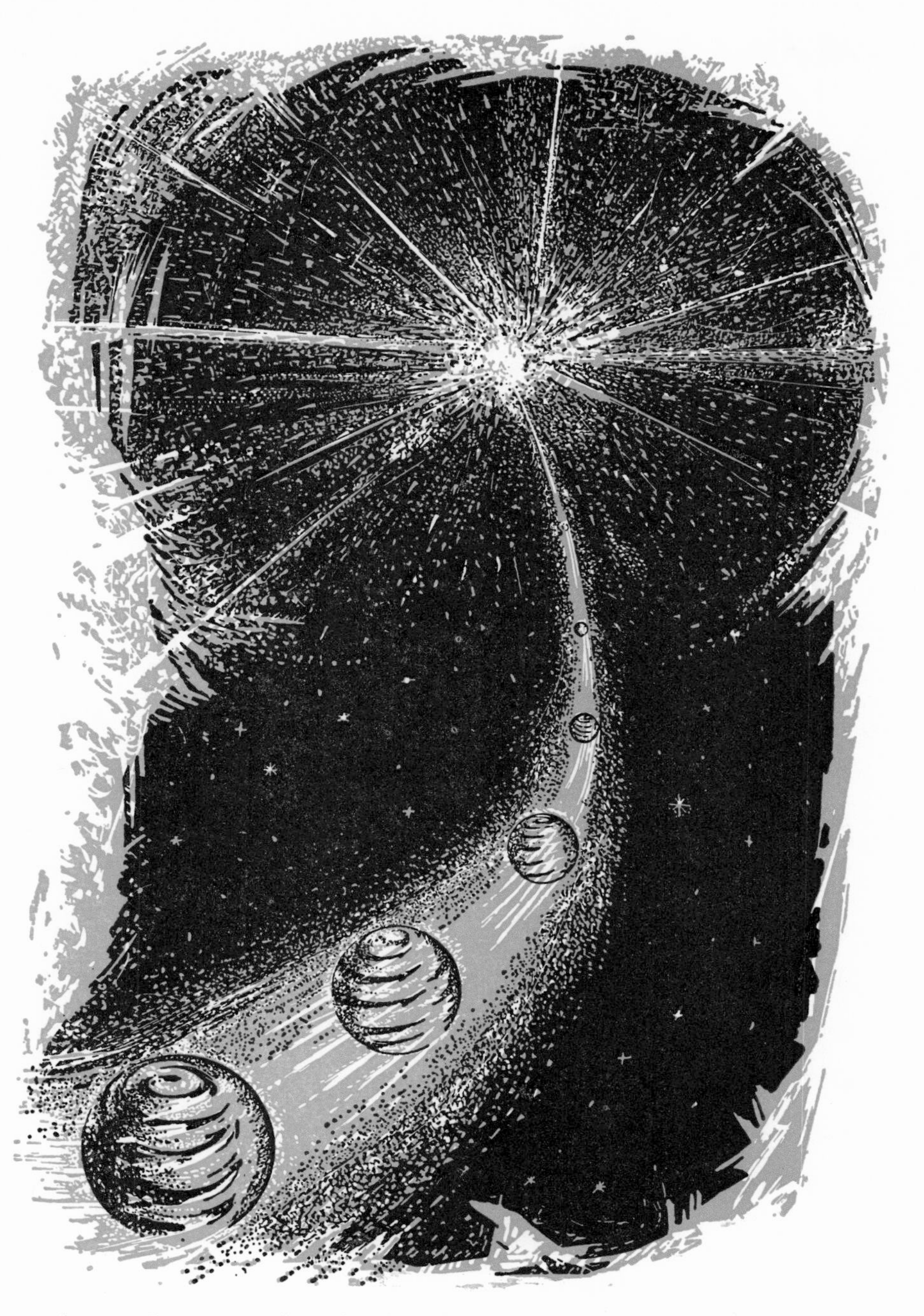

A nova is a giant that shrinks and shrinks until it finally explodes.

insides become exposed. After a while—generally a few months—the star settles back to normal. Then a few years later it is quite apt to go off the same way again.

Well, that's an ordinary nova. A super-nova is something even more violent. A super-nova has experienced the most violent thing that can ever happen anywhere in the whole universe. If you exploded a million million million million hydrogen bombs all at one time, that would make one super-nova explosion. For a super-nova doesn't fritter away its energy by shooting off bits of its surface now and again. It saves everything for one grand bang. When it happens, the explosion is over in about a minute. But in that minute perhaps nine-tenths of the star shoots off into space.

It is, of course, very exciting to watch a nova as it gets brighter and brighter and you picture what's happening up there millions of millions of miles away. But novae don't occur very often. And super-novae happen on the average only once in two or three centuries. You can, however, see other kinds of stars that vary in brightness and do it much more often.

One kind gets ten to a thousand times brighter every year or so. A lot of the huge red stars do that. We call such stars *long-period variables*. We don't understand them too well. What makes them dim and grow bright so rhythmically, like a pulse beating? Are there cyclical flare-ups there as on our sun? We don't know.

The Cepheid variables are altogether dependable stars. They change their brightness exactly on time. Some of the Cepheid variables change once a day. Some change once in several days. Some vary once a month.

This family gets its name from the first Cepheid to be discovered. It was the Delta star in the constellation Cepheus. But every star in the family is impressive.

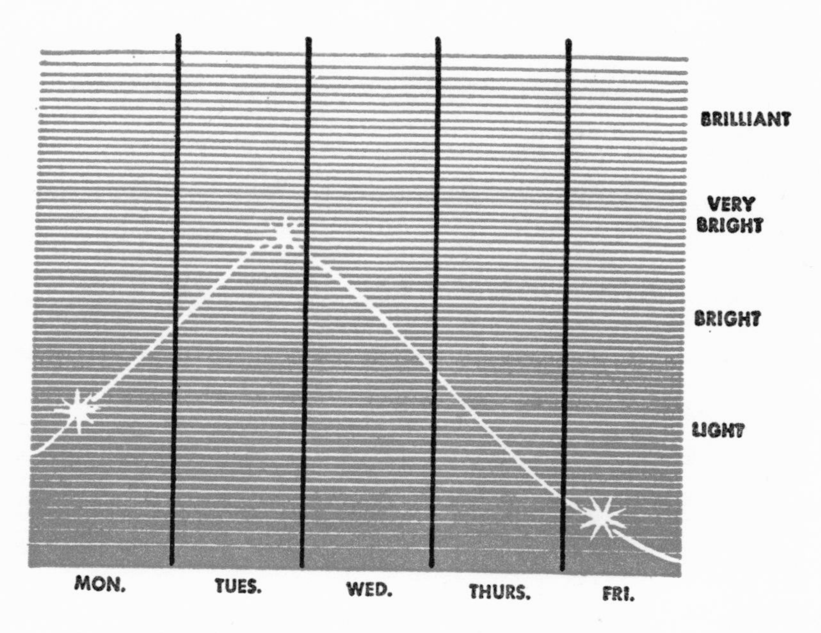

From day to day a single star may vary in brightness.

Every single star in the whole group is at least 100 times as bright as the sun, and many are several thousand times brighter. The most remarkable thing about them all, however, is not their brightness. It is that all the stars that have a one-day period are just alike—all of them are 100 times as luminous as the sun. All those that vary in a ten-day period are 2,000 times as powerful as the sun. While those that have a period of a month are brighter than 10,000 suns.

"But why," you want to know, "are the astronomers so fond of them?"

Remember how Bessel measured the distance to a star? First he sighted it from one side of our path around the sun and then six months later from the opposite side. Well, that way of measuring, as we said before, is accurate only for stars no farther than 100 light years away. But the Cepheid variables are all bright stars that can be seen very much farther away—and all of them fairly shout out their exact distance.

For see how it is. When we know a star's period, we can figure out how much brighter the star really is than the sun. And since we know that a star's brightness depends almost entirely on distance, we can tell at once how far away it is.

Think what that means to astronomers! The Cepheid variables do as much for us as the ten-league boots did for the man in the fairy story. Without them we would be forever tied to the "puny" region around the sun. Without them we could never explore confidently beyond a few hundred light years. The Cepheid variables are like brilliant milestones set up all over the sky. They shine out the distances even up to ten million light years. They give us wings to adventure "infinitely" far into space and know where we are.

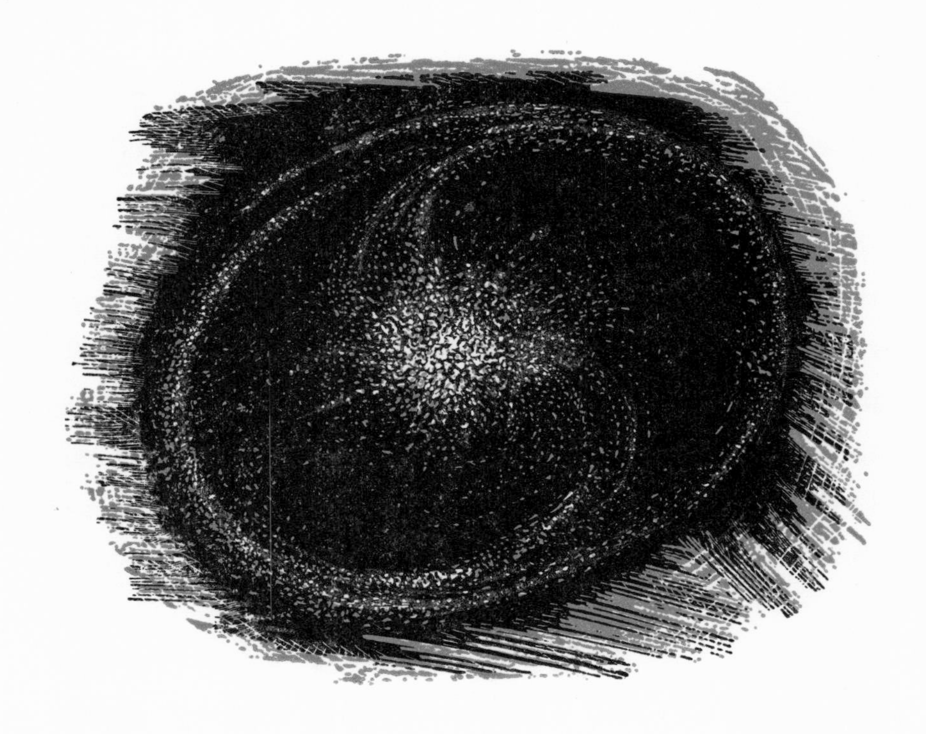

18.

Our Galaxy—and Others

Imagine an ant in a forest of countless trees. Imagine this ant trying to figure out the shape of the forest. It seems ridiculous, hopeless, impossible. And yet, man has solved a problem exactly of this order. He has figured out the shape and size of the gigantic "star city" in which we live—our galaxy. We call it ours because in the vast realm of space which the Cepheid variables have helped us conquer, there are about a thousand million galaxies besides our own.

What does the picture look like?

You might think because nearly everything in the sky seems to be a ball or a slightly flattened ball, that our galaxy is like that. But no. Our galaxy is like a tremendous pancake that is thicker at the center than at the edges. From where we are inside this pancake, we can't see far toward the center because of dust. But we can see out toward the edge, and the most important thing we see is the Milky Way. The Milky Way is how we see our galaxy from the inside. The fact that we find this luminous band of stars dividing the sky almost exactly in half tells us that we are about half way between the top and bottom of the pancake.

The size of our pancake is so tremendous that it is harder to picture than the distance to the stars. Our galaxy is something like 100,000 light years across. Out where we live—30,000 light years from the center and 20,000 from the edge—the pancake is thinner still. At the edge it drops off even more.

Now what is our pancake made of?

It is made of stars and dust and gases. There are 100,000 million stars in the pancake, most of the dim ones being in the band we call the Milky Way. The bulging center doubtless is the brightest part; for, though we can't see it to any extent, we have reason to think it is full of globular clusters. And brilliant globu-

If we could study a cross-section of our galaxy, we would see where the sun is located.

lar clusters surround the pancake as a halo. Out from the center of the galaxy the stars aren't distributed evenly. They form huge spiral arms in which there are enormously brilliant blue stars. Our sun and its neighbors lie near one of these great streams of stars.

The dust lies mostly in a layer right through the

middle of the pancake. That being just where we live, and some of the dust clouds being hundreds of light years across, you can see why we don't know too much about what's going on at the center. The dust gets in our way so that we see only about a hundredth part of the galaxy. There are holes or windows through which the astronomers see a portion of the central region.

As for the gas, it is nearly all hydrogen. Where it is close to some of the hottest stars, it glows like a neon advertising sign. The Great Nebula, or cloud, in the sword of Orion glows that way. It makes the middle star of the sword look fuzzy. In some regions when dust is close to stars, it also reflects enough light to be faintly visible. It's that way in the Pleiades, but there the nebula is much too dim to see with the naked eye.

Think now of huge clouds of gas many light years across, but don't think of the gas as being dense the way it is in the sun. A large matchbox full of material like the sun would contain 100 million million million million atoms. But in a matchbox of the gas between the stars, there would be only about 100 atoms. The gas between the stars is less dense than the most perfect vacuum we can make on earth. And yet there is enough of this gas in our galaxy to make another 100,000 million stars. It just points up how much more space there is than stars in the super-pancake that is our galaxy. The stars are terribly far apart.

The stars in our galaxy, of course, aren't standing still, for nothing in the sky stands still. If the moon stopped moving, it would fall to the earth. If the earth stopped moving, it would fall into the sun. And if the stars didn't move, the outer ones would fall into the center of the pancake. So our galaxy is a slowly whirling mass of stars spinning in space. It takes the sun, trailing its planets, 200 million years to go around the galaxy once. The distance is so vast that the sun has been around only twenty times since it was born.

It's not easy to get the picture, but luckily we've found a duplicate of our galaxy in the sky. We can turn our telescopes on it and see just what our star-city looks like.

Our model is one and a half million light years away, but you can see it as a blur even with the naked eye when you look on a winter's night through the stars of the constellation Andromeda. We call it galaxy in Andromeda or Messier 31—after the French astronomer who first catalogued it. He was looking for comets and made a list of all the fuzzy-looking things in the sky that people shouldn't mistake for comets. The Andromeda galaxy was Number 31 on his list.

At first glance, you don't see the resemblance—Messier 31 looks to be an oval, not a round pancake. But that is only because you see the galaxy tilted. Actually, it is in every respect a star city like our own. It is the same size. It has spiral arms unwinding—or is it winding? —from the same kind of bright center. It is as bright as our galaxy. And it has about as many stars. Some of its brightest stars flicker regularly like ours, spelling out how many times as luminous as the sun they really are. And that is a piece of luck. For it was by watching those flickering specks of light that we got the first measure of the distance of Messier 31. Those Cepheid variables, actually 1,000 times brighter than our sun, have to be one and a half million light years away to be as dim as we see them.

There are dust and gas clouds in the spiral arms just as there are in the arms of our galaxy. And out beyond and all around the spiral arms with their brilliant blue stars is a halo of globular clusters. In fact, the Andromeda galaxy or Messier 31 is our double and could pass for a photograph of our galaxy.

Astronomers have checked over Messier's list of 104

hazy objects that shouldn't be taken for comets and have found about a hundred of them to be galaxies. To these, our modern telescopes have added hundreds of millions more. Up to distances of a thousand million light years—and beyond—we keep finding more galaxies

More and more galaxies are being found.

and more. There seem to be just as many that far off as there are close by. So there is every reason to believe that out of our sight the galaxies go on and on—for a few thousand million light years at least.

Each galaxy is a star city. It may not be exactly like ours—it may have no spiral arms, no dust, no gas, and it may be smaller. Most of the galaxies are. But it is a whirling mass of millions of stars. It is a lonely world of light and motion sufficient unto itself, a world cut off by great stretches of dark, frigid, soundless space from other worlds just as lonely. Together they make what we call the visible universe—vast beyond belief.

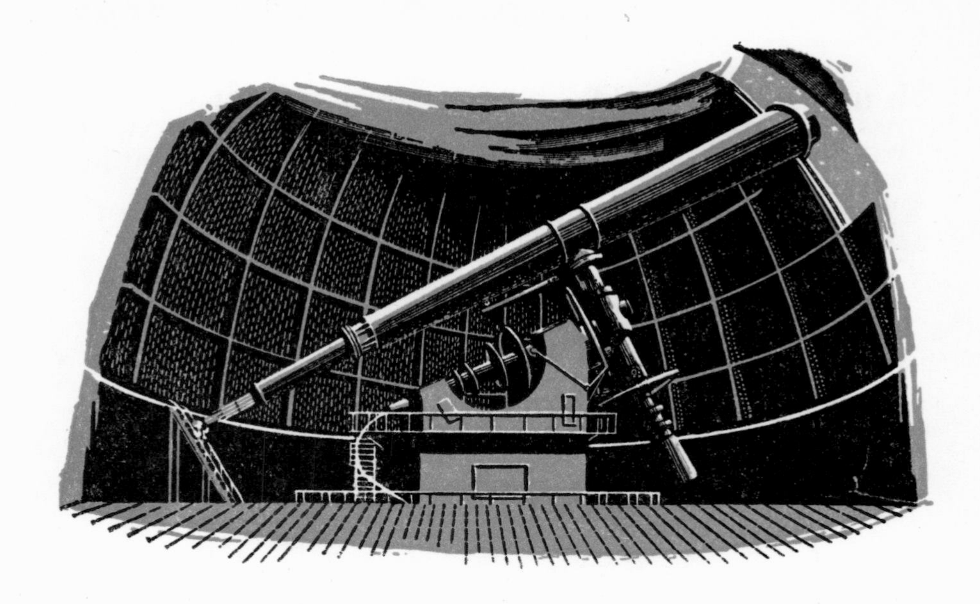

19.

Are There Other Worlds of Men?

Where did all the galaxies come from? How were the stars born?

Astronomers differ about a good many things, but this one thing they are agreed on. Everything we see in our universe today seems either to have started around four thousand million years ago or to have taken a new lease on life at that time. There were no stars then. Four thousand million years ago there were just immense clouds of atoms—masses of gas, that is.

Now clouds of gas don't stand still as anyone who

has watched smoke will appreciate. Clouds of gas swirl and churn and break up into eddies. And as they break up, the particles are drawn together by gravitation.

So it was with these original clouds. They condensed into blobs of whirling gas. As they rotated, the blobs slowly flattened out into pancakes and spirals. They became galaxies—infant galaxies, galaxies without any stars as yet. But the break-up and condensing didn't stop. The gas kept forming into blobs. In the spiral arms of the galaxies the blobs kept condensing into balls. And the more they condensed, the hotter they got on the inside. Finally, they got so hot that the hydrogen in their core started to turn into helium. The balls of gas began to glow—to radiate light, to send out heat. The stars were born.

They weren't all born at the same time. We know that some of the spendthrift stars are still going strong. This shows they must have been born later than some others. Otherwise they would have spent their light long ago. Stars were born at various times through all the 4,000 million years. Stars are being born today out of the gas that's left between the stars. They will continue to be born for thousands of millions of years to come. Stars will be born and stars will die.

Galaxies are formed out of whirling gases.

And now we come to the question that all the time has been in our minds. Do any of the stars have planets like our own and is there life on any of them?

There was a time when people refused even to explore such an idea. They were so self-centered they wanted to think they were the only creatures. We don't feel that way any more. Now we *want* to find other human beings on other planets. Are there such?

To answer that question we have to ask another one. Where did the planets come from? If they were formed in an accidental way, then we can't expect many stars to have planets. If, on the other hand, they were formed in a routine fashion, then many stars may have them. Astronomers aren't agreed on this matter at all.

Some believe the planets were born when a passing star came close to the sun. The star, they say, raised a tide in the sun and drew a cloud of gas out of it. Out of this cloud the planets condensed. If this is the way things happened, there can't be very many planets. For, as we said, the lanes of the sky are vastly wide and the chance of an accident or a near-accident is slight.

Others believe that no passing star was needed to produce the planets. The planets were made, they say, out of material thrown off by the sun. If that is the case, many stars may have planets.

Other astronomers, again, believe that the planets resulted from an explosion. They believe that the sun was not always alone as it now is, but that at one time it, too, had a companion. They believe this companion star was one of those spendthrifts that use up their capital fast and have a grand super-nova explosion. The planets, they believe, formed out of a bit of the exploded material that the sun managed to hold on to when the rest of the companion star blew away. If this is the way it happened, then there must be many stars with planets. For super-novae occur not only in our galaxy but in other galaxies. Throughout 4,000 million years a great many such explosions must have happened the universe around. One astronomer has figured out there must be in the Milky Way alone about 10 million planetary systems. And he estimates that life is possible on at least 100,000 of them.

It is an exciting thought. For scientists tell us that wherever life is possible, it does come into being. There may well be human beings on any number of planets. They may be looking up into the sky at this very moment and wondering whether there are beings like themselves on any other planets!

The Milky Way is our home in the sky.

Will we ever be able to reach them?

That is not likely. The distance to the moon we can span. The moon is only one and a half light seconds away. But the nearest star is over four light years away. Probably we can never span that distance, for traveling at the impossible speed of 186,000 miles a second, it would take us more than four years to get there. We are forever tied to the little region around the sun.

Only in our thought can we go farther. Man has taken one blow to his pride after another. He believed the earth was the center of the universe and that everything had been created on his account. He had to give that up. He found out that the sun is only an ordinary star among thousands of millions of other stars. He found that his galaxy is only one of a thousand million galaxies. Yet, for all his insignificance, he has reason to be proud. He has accomplished the seemingly impossible. Perhaps the greatest achievement of the human mind is understanding the stars.

Index

Index

Index